MALDIVES

TRAVEL GUIDE 2024

Where to Go, Insider Tips, Activities, Cultural Insights, and More for Your Perfect Getaway

Richard D. Orenstein

Copyright © 2024 Richard D. Orenstien

All rights reserved.

No part of this book may be reproduced or transmitted in any form or by any means, electronic or mechanical, including photocopying, recording, or by any information storage and retrieval system, without permission in writing from the author.

This book is a work of non-fiction. The views expressed are solely those of the author and do not necessarily reflect the views of the publisher, and the publisher hereby disclaims any responsibility for them.

Table of Contents

INTRODUCTION 7
CHAPTER 1 11
History of Maldives 11
   Reasons Why You Should Visit Maldives 13
   Planning Your Maldives Adventure: Choosing the Right Time to Visit 14
   Visa Requirements and Travel Documentation for Visiting Maldives 16
   Planning Your Trip 18
   Finding your way to Maldives 19
   Transportation Within Maldives 22
CHAPTER 2 25
Where to Stay in the Maldives 25
   Luxury Resorts and Overwater Bungalows 25
   Boutique Hotels and Guesthouses 27
   Hidden Gems for Budget Travellers 30
   Local Islands: 30
      Fulhadhoo Island: 31
      Thulusdhoo Island - The Surfing Haven: 31
      Biyadhoo Island - Snorkeler's Delight: 31
      Local Cuisine Exploration: 32

Public Ferries - The Budget-Friendly Commute: 32

Connecting with Locals: 32

Authentic Maldivian Hospitality 33

Family-Friendly Accommodations 35

CHAPTER 3 39

Exploring Maldivian Culture and History 39

Maldivian Traditions and Customs 39

Historical Landmarks and Museums 42

The Old Friday Mosque (Hukuru Miskiy) 43

National Museum of Maldives 43

Islamic Centre and Grand Friday Mosque 43

Maldives Islamic Centre Library 44

Utheemu Ganduvaru: The Historic Residence 44

Maldives Maritime Museum 44

Fua Mulaku Havitta 44

Medhu Ziyaaraiy: The Mysterious Tomb 45

CHAPTER 4 47

Unveiling Maldives' Natural Wonders 47

Pristine Beaches and Islands 47

Must-Visit Beaches 47

Hidden Islands to Explore 50

Snorkeling and Diving Spots 52

Marine Life Encounters 55
   Best Places for Shark Watching 55
   Coral Reefs and Vibrant Fish 58
   Dolphin and Whale Watching 60
Chapter 5 63
Activities for Different Traveler Types 63
   Solo Traveler's Guide 63
      Solo-Friendly Activities 63
      Safety Tips 66
      Meeting Other Travellers 68
   Couples Retreat 71
      Romantic Dinner Spots 71
      Private Island Escapes 74
   Family Adventures 77
      Kid-Friendly Attractions 77
      Family-Focused Excursions 79
      Educational Activities for Children 82
CHAPTER 6 87
Essential Things to Pack 87
   Clothing and Footwear 87
      Packing Tips for the Maldives Climate 87
      Beachwear Essentials 90

Snorkeling and Diving Gear 92
    Electronics and Gadgets 94
CHAPTER 7 95
Navigating Local Cuisine and Dining 95
    Traditional Maldivian Dishes 95
    Dietary Options and Restrictions 97
CHAPTER 8 101
Practical Tips for a Smooth Trip 101
    Health and Safety Guidelines 101
    Vaccinations and Health Precautions 101
    Sustainable and Responsible Tourism 103
        Eco-Friendly Practices 103
        Responsible Snorkeling and Diving 104
        Supporting Local Communities 106
CHAPTER 9 109
Language and Communication 109
    50 Useful Phrases for Travelers when visiting the Maldives: 110
CONCLUSION 115

INTRODUCTION

Set out on an incredible adventure across the breathtaking Maldivian beauties! This is more than simply a travel guide; it's your ticket to a life-changing experience, an exquisite tapestry adorned with the vivid hues of the Indian Ocean. With our this guide be ready to discover hidden jewels, take in breathtaking views, and delve into the rich tapestry of Maldivian history.

We'll be your travel companion as we lead you through the crystal-clear waters, immaculate beaches, and cultural gems that make the Maldives an absolute paradise on the pages that follow. Our guide is designed to suit all types of adventurers, whether you're a family looking for new adventures, a couple looking for romance, or a lone traveler.

Imagine yourself strolling along sandy beaches, experiencing the soft touch of a tropical wind, or diving into pristine seas brimming with marine life. Imagine exploring hidden islands, adopting regional traditions, and indulging in the mouthwatering tastes of Maldivian cuisine. This guide aims to provide readers an immersive experience of the Maldives, not merely a travel guide.

However, the Maldives' appeal goes beyond only their breathtaking scenery. We'll peel back the layers of

Maldivian history, taking you to historic sites, long-standing customs, and fascinating tales that have molded this archipelago nation. With every page flip, there's a new aspect of the Maldives to discover, from bustling marketplaces to tranquil mosques.

Discover helpful guidance on organizing your ideal vacation as you peruse these pages, from determining the best time to go to comprehending visa procedures and budgeting. We have everything you could possibly want, whether your dream is to live in an overwater bungalow or a charming guesthouse in the area.

This book is an invitation to make lasting experiences, not just a collection of facts. Discover travel experiences catered to your preferences, be they the excitement of independent discovery, the romance of a getaway for two, or the delight of family outings. Including food recommendations, health precautions, and packing advice, think of this book as your road map to a smooth and amazing trip.

Prepare yourself for a voyage across the Maldives. Allow yourself to be mesmerized by the cultural marvels, the coral reefs, and the blue oceans. This is the beginning of your journey; every page holds a revelation. Get ready to explore the Maldives' rich history, find hidden jewels, and take in the breathtaking scenery. Are you prepared for the voyage ahead?

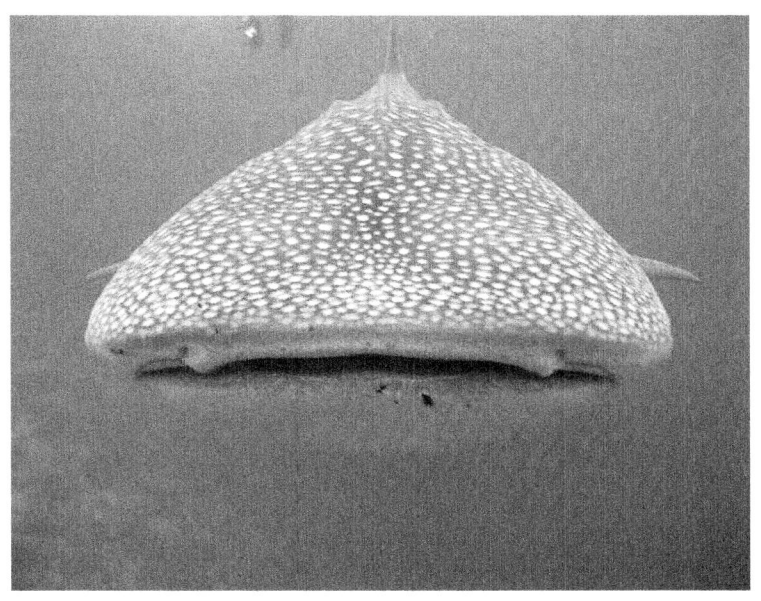

CHAPTER 1
History of Maldives

The Maldives is like a tropical dream come true, a chain of islands scattered across the Indian Ocean, where nature decided to show off its most brilliant colors. Picture this: 26 atolls, which are kind of like big groups of islands, with over 1,000 coral islands altogether. That's a lot of tiny slices of paradise!

Now, let's talk about the water – it's not just blue; it's the kind of blue that you only see in postcards. You can almost taste the saltiness in the air. The beaches? Soft as cotton candy. And guess what? These islands are all about luxury, with those fancy resorts and bungalows that sit right on top of the water. It's like having your own piece of the ocean all to yourself.

But the Maldives isn't just about pretty views; there's a whole bunch of sea creatures doing their thing beneath the waves. Think about colorful fish, playful dolphins, and even some sharks just doing their shark thing. If you're into exploring, grab a snorkel or some scuba gear – you'll be in for a treat.

Now, let's switch gears and talk about the people. The Maldivians are some of the friendliest folks you'll ever meet. They've got their own way of doing things, and they're proud of their culture. From their traditional clothes to the way they celebrate festivals, it's like taking a step back in time.

Oh, and did you know the Maldives has a history that goes way back? Like, ancient kings and queens kind of back. They've got cool stories about their past, and you can even visit museums and historic mosques to get a glimpse of it all.

Planning a trip here is like piecing together a puzzle. There's a right time for everything – whether you're looking for sunny days or avoiding rainy spells. And don't forget about visas; you need to sort out those papers before you start packing.

Talking about packing, bring your sunscreen, flip-flops, and maybe some fancy beachwear. Oh, and don't forget the snorkeling gear if you're up for some underwater adventures. But hey, we've got a whole chapter on what to pack, so no stress there.

Food? Get ready for a taste explosion. Maldivian dishes are like a burst of flavors in your mouth. From spicy curries to fresh seafood, your taste buds will be on a vacation of their own.

Whether you're a lone explorer, a couple looking for romance, or a family seeking some quality time, the Maldives has something for everyone. It's not just a place; it's an experience waiting to happen. So, buckle up, get ready to dip your toes in the warm sand, and let the Maldives work its magic on you. It's a journey you won't forget!

Reasons Why You Should Visit Maldives

Entering the Maldives seems like entering a surreal wonderland. It feels like you are living in a postcard, with smooth beaches and crystal blue sea. Some of the resorts are situated directly on the water, making them more than simply fancy hotels. It's quite unique to have your own place in the midst of the ocean.

The Maldives is a sea life display underwater. It's an explorer's paradise, with colorful fish, lively dolphins, and even some sharks. It seems as if you are diving or snorkeling beneath the waters in a whole different universe.

The people of the Maldives are what make them unique. Maldivians take great pride in their culture and are kind. A glimpse of their ancestry may be experienced through traditional attire and vibrant festivals.

The Maldives has old stories to share with history buffs. These islands were originally controlled by kings and queens, and the historic mosques and museums include artifacts from that era.

It is simple to plan your trip. Everything has its own time, and obtaining visas in advance is essential. It's easy to pack: consider sunglasses, flip-flops, and a cap. All the necessities are included in the guide.

Food from the Maldives is a taste explosion. Every meal, whether it's fresh seafood or hot curries, is a culinary adventure.

There's something for everyone in the Maldives, be it a family, a couple, or a lone visitor. It's an experience waiting to happen, not simply a location. So prepare to bury your toes in the warm sand and allow the Maldives' allure to create lifelong memories. It seems to be an adventure that will never be forgotten.

Planning Your Maldives Adventure: Choosing the Right Time to Visit

Determining the ideal time for your journey to the Maldives involves navigating the intricacies of its distinct seasons. Let's delve into this topic with simplicity.

The Maldives experiences two main seasons: the dry season, stretching from November to April, and the wet season, spanning from May to October. During the dry season, envision an enchanting setting with the sun taking the spotlight and the skies portraying a seamless canvas of blue. It's a time when nature herself seems to encourage you to explore the sandy beaches and delve into the wonders beneath the ocean's surface.

Conversely, the wet season introduces sporadic rain showers from May to October, offering a refreshing touch to the landscape. While the name may imply a continuous downpour, it's more like nature's way of keeping the surroundings lush and vibrant. A notable aspect of the wet season is its potential for more budget-friendly options, with hotels and amenities occasionally offering more economical deals.

However, nature's whims can introduce surprises, like an unexpected raindrop during the dry season or a burst of sunshine amid the wet season. It's as if the natural world likes to keep things interesting and defy expectations.

When contemplating the timing of your Maldivian adventure, consider your preferences. If you savor clear, sunny days, the dry season is tailor-made for you. On the other hand, if you don't mind a sprinkle of rain and are attracted by the prospect of potential savings, the wet season could align with your preferences. Consulting the weather forecast and packing accordingly are integral steps in preparing for your Maldives experience.

In essence, the best time to visit the Maldives depends on the atmosphere you seek. Whether it's the warmth of the dry season or the refreshing interludes of the wet season, each moment offers a unique facet of the Maldives' allure. It's about finding the temporal tapestry that aligns with your travel aspirations, ensuring that your journey to this tropical haven becomes a seamless and captivating experience.

Visa Requirements and Travel Documentation for Visiting Maldives

Understanding the necessary travel documentation for a visit to the Maldives is crucial for a smooth journey. Let's delve into this topic, ensuring clarity for readers of all backgrounds.

First and foremost, your passport is your ticket to international travel. Ensure that it is valid for at least six months from your planned date of return. This simple detail can prevent any last-minute travel disruptions.

When it comes to visas, the Maldives simplifies the process for short-term visitors. If your stay is less than 30 days, you generally don't need to obtain a visa in advance. It's a welcoming gesture, making it easier for short-term travelers to explore the beauty of the Maldives.

The Maldives operates on a visa-on-arrival system, allowing seamless entry for many visitors. Upon arrival, travelers are required to fill out an arrival card, a straightforward process. Subsequently, a 30-day visa is stamped onto the passport, allowing for a hassle-free commencement of the journey.

For those planning a longer stay beyond the initial 30 days, it's advisable to check in with Maldivian immigration authorities. They can provide guidance on the necessary steps to extend your visit. These immigration officials are akin to wizards behind the scenes, helping travelers navigate the intricacies of an extended stay.

While the Maldives generally embraces a relaxed visa policy, it's imperative to adhere to local laws and regulations. Respecting these guidelines ensures a harmonious stay and prevents any unnecessary complications.

A practical tip for all travelers is to keep copies of essential documents. This precautionary measure, like having a backup plan, can prove invaluable in unforeseen situations.

To sum it up – a valid passport, a simple arrival card, and a seamless visa-on-arrival process for shorter stays. For longer visits, a friendly conversation with immigration authorities is in order. Respect the rules, keep copies of your documents, and you're set for a worry-free exploration of the Maldives. This straightforward approach ensures that travelers, regardless of their familiarity with international travel, can embark on their Maldivian adventure with confidence and ease.

Planning Your Trip

Understanding how to budget for a trip to the Maldives is essential for a smooth and enjoyable experience. Let's explore this topic in simple terms, ensuring accessibility for all readers.

Firstly, let's talk about the local currency in the Maldives, which is the Maldivian Rufiyaa (MVR). However, US dollars are widely accepted, and many transactions, especially in tourist areas, are conducted in dollars. It's like having a dual currency system that gives visitors flexibility.

When budgeting for your trip, consider the estimated costs for accommodation, meals, transportation, and activities. Accommodation costs can vary widely, ranging from budget guesthouses to luxurious overwater bungalows. Similarly, dining expenses can differ based on your choice of restaurants – from local eateries to upscale dining establishments.

Transportation costs include inter-island transfers and any excursions you plan to undertake. These costs can vary, so it's beneficial to research and plan accordingly. Activities such as water sports, island hopping, or cultural experiences may also contribute to your overall expenses.

For currency exchange, it's advisable to do so at official exchange counters, banks, or your accommodation. Be aware of the exchange rates to ensure you get a fair deal.

Some areas might accept credit cards, but it's wise to carry cash for places that might not have card facilities.

Managing expenses involves keeping track of your spending. Consider creating a daily budget, and keep an eye on your expenditures to avoid any surprises. Utilize local transportation options like ferries for a budget-friendly way to explore the islands.

Remember that budgeting is about finding a balance between enjoying your trip and being mindful of your spending. By planning ahead and staying conscious of your expenses, you can make the most of your Maldivian adventure without breaking the bank. It's like navigating the financial aspect of your journey with ease, ensuring that your focus remains on the beauty and experiences the Maldives has to offer.

Finding your way to Maldives

Embarking on the remarkable journey to the Maldives involves a series of thoughtful considerations to ensure a voyage that is both seamless and gratifying. Let's delve into this process with comprehensive detail while maintaining a language that resonates with readers from all walks of life.

To commence your expedition, securing a flight to Malé International Airport serves as the initial step. This pivotal airport functions as the primary gateway to the Maldives, with various airlines providing direct or connecting flights from diverse corners of the globe. This stage mirrors the strategic selection of the starting point of your adventure, acting as the conduit to the mesmerizing archipelago.

Upon landing at Malé International Airport, the subsequent task revolves around arranging transportation to your designated island haven. Inter-island travel commonly takes the form of domestic flights, seaplanes, or speedboats. The choice of transport parallels the selection of a tailored mode that adeptly connects the dots between islands, each boasting its unique allure.

For those opting for the luxury of resort accommodations, many establishments streamline the process by organizing seaplane or speedboat transfers directly from the airport. This bespoke service mirrors the provision of a seamless journey, transitioning you effortlessly from the airport hub to your chosen island retreat.

Conversely, if your inclination leans towards exploring local islands or guesthouses, the public ferry system or privately arranged speedboat transfers become viable options. This avenue offers a more immersive encounter, affording you the opportunity to absorb local life and picturesque scenery as you traverse the waters between islands.

A fundamental grasp of the Maldives' geography proves advantageous when selecting your desired destination. The archipelago comprises over 1,000 coral islands clustered in 26 atolls, forming a complex yet enchanting mosaic. Navigating this natural tapestry becomes akin to steering through a canvas where each island unveils its distinct character.

Effective communication emerges as a critical component during your journey. Fortunately, English serves as a widely spoken language in tourist hubs, facilitating seamless interactions with locals and facilitating inquiries. This linguistic commonality acts as a bridge, fostering effective communication and understanding across cultural boundaries.

Orchestrating your voyage to the Maldives entails a meticulous orchestration of steps – from booking your flight to selecting the optimal mode of inter-island transportation. Whether drawn to the convenience of resort transfers or the immersive charm of local island travel, the Maldives offers a diverse array of options tailored to cater to your individual preferences. It's akin to sculpting a bespoke journey that aligns precisely with your travel aspirations, ensuring that each leg of the expedition contributes to an indelible and enriching experience in this tropical haven.

Transportation Within Maldives

Navigating the enchanting islands of the Maldives involves exploring various transportation options, each contributing to the unique tapestry of this tropical paradise. Let's delve into these modes of travel with comprehensive details.

Inter-Island Travel: The Maldives, comprising over 1,000 coral islands grouped in 26 atolls, presents a captivating yet intricate geography. To traverse this archipelago, inter-island travel is facilitated through domestic flights, seaplanes, or speedboats. Domestic flights connect major hubs, offering a swift and convenient mode of transportation. Seaplanes provide an aerial spectacle, offering a unique vantage point as they land on the azure waters near your chosen island. Speedboats cater to those seeking a more direct and intimate waterborne journey, efficiently navigating the crystalline channels between islands.

Resort Transfers: For those indulging in the luxury of resort accommodations, seamless transfers are often arranged by the establishments. These can involve seaplanes or speedboats, providing guests with a tailored and hassle-free transition from the main airport to the secluded retreat. These resort transfers not only enhance the overall experience but also showcase the breathtaking beauty of the Maldivian seascape.

Local Island Exploration: Travelers keen on immersing themselves in local culture can utilize public ferries and privately arranged speedboat transfers for island hopping. Public ferries, although less luxurious, provide an authentic experience, allowing you to witness daily life as you journey between local islands. Privately arranged speedboats offer a more personalized touch, enabling efficient and comfortable travel.

Communication and Local Currency: Communication in the Maldives is primarily conducted in English, especially in tourist areas, making interactions with locals and navigating transportation options more straightforward. Additionally, it's essential to have local currency, the Maldivian Rufiyaa (MVR), for small transactions and purchases. While U.S. dollars are widely accepted, understanding the local currency adds a layer of convenience.

Transportation within the Maldives is a multifaceted aspect of the overall travel experience. The diverse options, whether soaring over atolls in a seaplane, feeling the sea breeze on a speedboat, or embarking on a cultural journey via public ferries, contribute to the richness of exploring this tropical haven. Understanding these transportation modes ensures that travelers can tailor their journey to align with their preferences, creating an immersive and fulfilling Maldivian adventure.

CHAPTER 2
Where to Stay in the Maldives

Nestled amidst the azure waters of the Indian Ocean, the Maldives beckons with its pristine beauty and a plethora of islands, each offering a unique slice of paradise. As you embark on the exciting journey of planning your stay in this tropical haven, understanding the diverse accommodation options becomes paramount. In this chapter, we delve into the intricacies of "Where to Stay in the Maldives," exploring the varied choices that cater to different preferences and budgets.

Luxury Resorts and Overwater Bungalows

In the tapestry of the Maldives' allure, luxury resorts and their iconic overwater bungalows stand as defining features, weaving an enchanting narrative of opulence against the backdrop of the Indian Ocean.

The Allure of Overwater Bungalows: Picture a secluded haven suspended above the cerulean waters – this is the essence of overwater bungalows. These distinctive accommodations extend over the lagoon, providing a seamless blend of luxury and nature. The allure lies not just in the lavish interiors but in the immersive experience of waking up to the gentle caress of ocean breezes and the rhythmic lull of waves beneath your private abode.

Design and Architecture: Architecturally, overwater bungalows showcase an elegant blend of traditional Maldivian craftsmanship and modern design. Thatched roofs and wooden accents pay homage to the local aesthetic, while expansive windows and private decks invite the mesmerizing surroundings into your living space. The design ethos is a celebration of harmony – an invitation to bask in the natural splendor that envelops these exquisite retreats.

Luxury Resorts as Sanctuaries: Luxury resorts in the Maldives transcend mere accommodation; they are sanctuaries of unparalleled extravagance. These havens are strategically located on private islands, ensuring seclusion and exclusivity. Guests are welcomed into a world where personalized service, culinary delights, and recreational activities are meticulously curated to elevate every aspect of their stay.

Culinary Experiences: A stay in a luxury resort extends beyond the physical abode. Culinary experiences become a journey of their own, with an array of dining options ranging from intimate beachfront dinners to underwater restaurants. Each meal is a gastronomic symphony, fusing global flavors with the freshest local ingredients.

Recreational Paradises: From private infinity pools to world-class spas, luxury resorts in the Maldives are designed as recreational paradises. Dive into the vibrant coral reefs, embark on sunset cruises, or simply unwind on pristine beaches – every moment is an opportunity to immerse yourself in the captivating surroundings.

Sustainability and Conservation: Many luxury resorts in the Maldives embrace sustainable practices and environmental conservation. Efforts to preserve the delicate marine ecosystems include coral restoration projects, waste reduction initiatives, and a commitment to renewable energy sources. These endeavors ensure that the beauty that captivates visitors today endures for generations to come.

Lluxury resorts and overwater bungalows in the Maldives transcend the realm of accommodation. They are gateways to a world where extravagance harmonizes with nature, where every detail is a testament to the unique allure of this tropical paradise. As we delve into the realms of opulence and natural beauty, it becomes evident that these exclusive retreats are not just places to stay – they are immersive experiences that redefine the art of indulgence against the canvas of the Maldivian seascape.

Boutique Hotels and Guesthouses

In the enchanting archipelago of the Maldives, boutique hotels and guesthouses emerge as understated gems, offering a more intimate and culturally immersive experience for discerning travelers.

Boutique Hotels: Boutique hotels in the Maldives are characterized by their unique identity and personalized service. Nestled on both local islands and private islets, these establishments exude a distinct charm, often blending modern comforts with local aesthetics. The emphasis here is on creating an atmosphere of exclusivity, where guests feel not only accommodated but truly embraced by the distinctive ambiance.

Intimate Settings: Unlike larger resorts, boutique hotels favor a more intimate setting, fostering a sense of familiarity and connection. With fewer rooms, these establishments can offer a more personalized approach, ensuring that every guest receives individual attention. The result is an environment where travelers can feel like cherished guests rather than mere visitors.

Local Cultural Immersion: One of the notable aspects of boutique hotels in the Maldives is their proximity to local communities. Many are situated on inhabited islands, providing guests with the opportunity to immerse themselves in the authentic Maldivian way of life. From sampling local delicacies to engaging with the friendly locals, staying in a boutique hotel becomes a cultural exploration.

Design Elegance: The design ethos of boutique hotels often reflects a tasteful blend of contemporary elements and traditional Maldivian influences. Thatched roofs, open-air spaces, and locally inspired decor create an inviting ambiance that resonates with the natural beauty of the surroundings. Each boutique hotel is a carefully curated space, where aesthetics play a crucial role in enhancing the overall guest experience.

Guesthouses: Guesthouses, synonymous with warmth and simplicity, provide an alternative accommodation option for those seeking a more budget-friendly yet authentic stay in the Maldives. These establishments, often run by local families, offer a glimpse into Maldivian hospitality on inhabited islands.

Local Connection: Choosing a guesthouse means more than just securing a place to stay; it signifies a connection to the local community. Guests have the chance to interact with residents, share stories, and gain insights into the daily life of Maldivians. It's a unique opportunity to go beyond the typical tourist experience and form genuine connections.

Affordability: A notable advantage of guesthouses is their affordability, making the Maldives accessible to a broader range of travelers. Without compromising on the essence of a genuine Maldivian experience, guests can enjoy comfortable lodgings and warm hospitality without breaking the bank.

Boutique hotels and guesthouses in the Maldives offer a distinctive avenue for travelers to savor the beauty of the islands. Whether opting for the curated luxury of a boutique hotel or the genuine warmth of a guesthouse, each stay promises an authentic encounter with the Maldivian way of life. These accommodations stand as testaments to the diversity of options available, ensuring that every traveler can find a home away from home in this tropical paradise.

Hidden Gems for Budget Travellers

In the expansive canvas of the Maldives, often perceived as a haven for luxury travel, lies a trove of hidden gems awaiting discovery by budget-conscious travelers. This section aims to illuminate the pathways to these uncharted yet enchanting corners of the archipelago, where affordability seamlessly intertwines with the captivating beauty of this tropical paradise.

Local Islands: Hidden gems for budget travelers in the Maldives often manifest in the form of local islands. Away from the well-trodden paths of resort-dominated atolls, these islands offer a more authentic and affordable experience. Guesthouses, scattered across these local havens, provide comfortable accommodations, allowing travelers to immerse themselves in the rhythm of Maldivian daily life.

Fulhadhoo Island: One such hidden gem is Fulhadhoo Island, an epitome of tranquility and pristine beauty. Accessible by public ferry, this coral island boasts budget-friendly guesthouses and a serene ambiance. White sandy beaches, crystal-clear lagoons, and vibrant coral reefs await those seeking an unspoiled paradise without breaking the bank.

Thulusdhoo Island - The Surfing Haven: For budget travelers with a penchant for adventure, Thulusdhoo Island beckons. Known as the local hub for surf enthusiasts, this hidden gem offers affordable guesthouses and a vibrant local atmosphere. Beyond the captivating waves, Thulusdhoo unveils a cultural tapestry with traditional craftsmanship, including the renowned Maldivian surfboard-making industry.

Biyadhoo Island - Snorkeler's Delight: Biyadhoo Island, nestled within South Malé Atoll, stands as a hidden haven for snorkeling enthusiasts on a budget. This tranquil island accommodates budget-friendly options, allowing visitors to explore the vibrant marine life just steps away from the shoreline. The coral gardens surrounding Biyadhoo present an underwater spectacle accessible to budget-conscious travelers.

Local Cuisine Exploration: A hidden gem of budget travel is the opportunity to savor Maldivian cuisine authentically. Local eateries on inhabited islands offer a delectable array of traditional dishes at affordable prices. Delight in flavorsome curries, freshly caught seafood, and tropical fruits, experiencing the genuine taste of the Maldives without straining your wallet.

Public Ferries - The Budget-Friendly Commute: Navigating between islands is an adventure in itself, and budget travelers can harness the cost-effective charm of public ferries. These communal vessels connect various local islands, providing an opportunity to witness the Maldivian seascape while keeping transportation expenses in check.

Connecting with Locals: An intrinsic hidden gem lies in the warmth of Maldivian hospitality. Engaging with locals, participating in community events, and embracing the cultural nuances create priceless memories for budget travelers. These authentic connections offer a richer understanding of the Maldivian way of life, transcending the conventional tourist experience.

The Maldives, often perceived as an exclusive retreat, harbors hidden gems that cater to budget-conscious travelers. From local islands with affordable guesthouses to unexplored corners where nature unfolds its untouched beauty, these gems present an alternative narrative of the

Maldives. By embracing local experiences, affordable accommodations, and the genuine warmth of Maldivian hospitality, budget travelers can uncover the true essence of this tropical paradise without compromising on the enchantment that defines the Maldivian experience.

Authentic Maldivian Hospitality

In the heart of the Maldives, beyond the pristine beaches and turquoise waters, lies a cornerstone of the Maldivian experience: authentic hospitality. This section endeavors to unravel the threads of this hospitality tapestry, where warmth, sincerity, and a genuine sense of connection define the essence of welcoming visitors to this tropical paradise.

Personalized Welcome: Authentic Maldivian hospitality extends beyond the conventional. It begins with a personalized welcome that transcends formalities, offering visitors a sense of being not just guests but cherished members of the community. This warm reception sets the tone for a stay infused with genuine care and consideration.

Community Connection: A distinctive feature of Maldivian hospitality is the connection to the local community. Whether staying on a local island or interacting with islanders during excursions, visitors have the opportunity to engage with Maldivians in their everyday lives. This immersion creates a unique bond, allowing travelers to experience the culture and traditions firsthand.

Guesthouses and Local Accommodations: Choosing guesthouses on local islands unveils a facet of Maldivian hospitality that goes beyond luxury resorts. Run by local families, these accommodations offer a more intimate and authentic experience. Hosts often share insights into Maldivian life, introduce guests to local customs, and ensure that each visitor feels not merely accommodated but genuinely welcomed.

Culinary Delights: A significant aspect of Maldivian hospitality unfolds around the dining table. Traditional Maldivian cuisine, often prepared with fresh, locally sourced ingredients, becomes a gateway to the culture. Visitors are welcomed to savor flavorsome curries, tropical fruits, and seafood, providing not just a meal but an immersive journey into Maldivian culinary traditions.

Friendly Islanders: Maldivians are renowned for their friendliness, and this amiable nature extends to interactions with visitors. Islanders, whether guiding snorkeling excursions, leading island tours, or simply engaging in conversations, radiate warmth. This genuine friendliness transforms every encounter into a memorable experience, leaving an indelible mark on the traveler's journey.

Celebrating Festivities: Authentic Maldivian hospitality embraces the celebration of local festivities. Visitors may have the opportunity to partake in traditional events, such as Bodu Eid or the Maldives Islamic New Year. These celebrations provide a glimpse into the cultural richness of the Maldives, fostering a sense of inclusion and shared joy.

Environmental Stewardship: In addition to personal connections, authentic Maldivian hospitality often aligns with a commitment to environmental stewardship. Many accommodations, from luxury resorts to guesthouses, engage in eco-friendly practices, reflecting a collective effort to preserve the pristine beauty of the islands for future generations.

Authentic Maldivian hospitality is a nuanced and genuine expression that elevates a visit to the Maldives beyond a mere vacation. It is an invitation to be part of a community, to embrace cultural nuances, and to forge connections that endure beyond the shores of this enchanting archipelago. As travelers experience the heartfelt welcome and genuine warmth of the Maldivian people, they become not just spectators but integral participants in a hospitality narrative that leaves an indelible mark on the soul.

Family-Friendly Accommodations

In the enchanting archipelago of the Maldives, the concept of family-friendly accommodations weaves a thoughtful narrative that caters to the diverse needs of travelers with children.

Spacious Villas and Suites: Family-friendly accommodations in the Maldives often feature spacious villas or suites designed to provide ample room for parents and children. These well-appointed living spaces allow families to enjoy their private retreats, fostering a sense of comfort and relaxation.

Kid-Friendly Amenities: Considerate of younger guests, family-friendly resorts incorporate kid-friendly amenities that enhance the overall experience for children. From dedicated play areas and splash pools to engaging activities, these thoughtful additions cater to the unique needs and preferences of younger travelers.

Supervised Kids' Clubs: Many family-friendly resorts in the Maldives offer supervised kids' clubs, providing a safe and entertaining environment for children to engage in age-appropriate activities. These clubs often organize creative workshops, games, and cultural experiences, ensuring that children have their own delightful adventures while parents enjoy moments of relaxation.

Family-Oriented Dining: Family-friendly accommodations understand the importance of hassle-free dining experiences. Buffet-style meals, diverse menu options, and flexible dining hours cater to the varied tastes and schedules of families, making mealtimes enjoyable and stress-free.

Water and Adventure Activities: Beyond the sandy shores, family-friendly accommodations in the Maldives offer an array of water and adventure activities suitable for all ages. Snorkeling excursions, dolphin watching, and family-friendly water sports provide opportunities for shared experiences, creating lasting memories for parents and children alike.

Educational and Cultural Activities: To enrich the family vacation experience, some family-friendly resorts in the Maldives incorporate educational and cultural activities. Guided marine biology sessions, local island visits, or storytelling sessions centered around Maldivian folklore contribute to a holistic and educational journey for young minds.

Flexible Childcare Services: Recognizing that parents may wish to indulge in some alone time, family-friendly accommodations often offer flexible childcare services. Trained staff members can look after children, ensuring their safety and enjoyment while parents indulge in spa treatments, romantic dinners, or other activities.

Safety Measures: Family-friendly accommodations prioritize safety, implementing measures such as secure pool areas, childproofing in villas, and lifeguards on duty at designated swimming spots. These precautions contribute to a worry-free environment, allowing families to focus on creating cherished moments together.

Family-friendly accommodations in the Maldives are designed to harmonize luxury with practicality, ensuring that families can immerse themselves in the beauty of this tropical paradise while enjoying the convenience and comfort tailored to their unique needs. Whether it's the spacious accommodations, kid-friendly amenities, or a thoughtful array of activities, these accommodations stand as gateways to unforgettable family vacations in one of the world's most stunning destinations.

CHAPTER 3
Exploring Maldivian Culture and History

Embarking on a journey through the Maldives is not merely a traverse across its crystalline waters and sandy shores; it is an immersion into a rich tapestry of culture and history that has shaped the identity of these breathtaking islands. In this chapter, we delve into the vibrant heritage that breathes life into the Maldives, unraveling the threads of a narrative that spans centuries and reflects the resilience and distinctiveness of the Maldivian people.

Maldivian Traditions and Customs

In the heart of the Maldives, beyond the azure waters and beneath the gentle sway of palm fronds, lie the timeless traditions and customs that define the cultural fabric of this enchanting archipelago.

Dhivehi Raajje: The Land of Maldivians: The Maldives, known locally as Dhivehi Raajje, embraces a cultural heritage steeped in centuries-old traditions. The term 'Dhivehi' signifies both the nation's language and its people, reflecting a unity that transcends the islands' geographical expanse.

Bodu Beru: The Rhythmic Heartbeat: Central to Maldivian traditions is the rhythmic beat of the Bodu Beru drums. This traditional drumming, characterized by its resonant tones and vibrant energy, serves as a cultural emblem. Bodu Beru performances, often accompanied by spirited dance, are a celebration of community, echoing the collective spirit that defines Maldivian gatherings.

Bajau: Artistry in Motion: The Bajau, a traditional dance form, embodies the graceful movements and vibrant colors of Maldivian culture. Dancers, adorned in elaborate costumes, sway to melodic tunes, creating a visual spectacle that encapsulates the artistic expression deeply ingrained in Maldivian traditions.

Thaana Script: Dhivehi Language Unveiled: The Dhivehi language, written in the unique Thaana script, stands as a linguistic treasure. This script, devised in the 16th century, serves as a testament to the Maldivian people's commitment to preserving their cultural identity through written expression.

Cultural Influences: The Crossroads of Traditions: Maldivian traditions bear the imprints of diverse cultural influences. Shaped by centuries of interactions with Arab, African, and South Asian traders, the Maldives has become a crossroads of cultural exchange. The result is a fusion of traditions that resonate with the islands' geographic location at the heart of the Indian Ocean.

Fuvahmulah: The Island of Unique Customs: Fuvahmulah, a unique atoll in the Maldives, stands as a testament to the diversity of Maldivian traditions. Known for its distinct dialect, customs, and folklore, Fuvahmulah offers a glimpse into the rich tapestry of island life, showcasing how traditions can evolve in varied settings.

Bodu Mas: The Grand Mosque: The Islamic faith, deeply embedded in Maldivian traditions, finds expression in the Bodu Mas (Grand Mosque). The architectural marvel of this mosque, adorned with intricate carvings, stands as a symbol of religious devotion and cultural aesthetics.

Eid Celebrations: Joyous Communal Festivities: Eid al-Fitr and Eid al-Adha, significant Islamic celebrations, bring communities together in joyous festivities. Families and friends gather to share meals, exchange gifts, and express gratitude, creating a sense of unity that transcends individual households.

Dhoni: Sailing Through Time: The traditional Maldivian boat, the Dhoni, is more than a vessel; it is an embodiment of seafaring heritage. Used for fishing and transportation, the Dhoni reflects the islanders' connection to the vast expanse of the Indian Ocean, a connection that has sustained generations of Maldivians.

Maldivian Hospitality: A Cultural Pillar: Embedded in Maldivian customs is the warmth of hospitality. Visitors are welcomed with open hearts, invited to share in local customs, and treated as honored guests. This hospitality, deeply ingrained in the cultural ethos, exemplifies the Maldivian spirit of generosity and kindness.

The traditions and customs of the Maldives are an intricate weave of history, artistry, and cultural exchange. As you navigate through the pages of this exploration, envision the vibrant Bodu Beru performances, feel the rhythmic beats of traditions passed through generations, and immerse yourself in the timeless allure of Maldivian culture. It is an invitation to understand, appreciate, and celebrate the cultural nuances that make the Maldives not just a destination but a living testament to the resilience and richness of human traditions.

Historical Landmarks and Museums

Within the serene embrace of the Maldives, where turquoise waters gently lap against pristine shores, there lies a tapestry of historical landmarks and museums that whispers tales of the archipelago's storied past. This detailed exploration invites you to traverse through time, discovering the remnants of ancient civilizations and the cultural gems that weave together the narrative of the Maldives' historical heritage.

The Old Friday Mosque (Hukuru Miskiy)

As a testament to the enduring beauty of Maldivian craftsmanship, the Old Friday Mosque, locally known as Hukuru Miskiy, stands as a living monument. Constructed in 1658, this coral stone mosque showcases intricate carvings and traditional Maldivian artistry. Its architectural charm reflects the influence of South Asian, Arab, and Maldivian craftsmanship, creating a captivating blend that resonates with the island's rich history.

National Museum of Maldives

Located in the capital city of Malé, the National Museum is a repository of Maldivian heritage. Opened in 1952, this museum houses an extensive collection of artifacts spanning the nation's history. From ancient weaponry and royal regalia to intricately carved wooden objects, the exhibits provide a chronological journey through the Maldives' cultural evolution.

Islamic Centre and Grand Friday Mosque

An iconic silhouette gracing the Malé skyline, the Islamic Centre and Grand Friday Mosque epitomize the nation's deep-rooted Islamic heritage. The mosque, completed in 1984, is a modern architectural marvel, featuring a golden dome and intricate Islamic geometric patterns. It stands not only as a place of worship but also as a symbol of the Maldives' commitment to its religious identity.

Maldives Islamic Centre Library
Adjacent to the Grand Friday Mosque, the Maldives Islamic Centre Library serves as a haven for literature enthusiasts and researchers alike. The library houses a vast collection of Islamic texts, historical manuscripts, and publications, fostering an intellectual space that reflects the nation's scholarly pursuits.

Utheemu Ganduvaru: The Historic Residence
Stepping onto the island of Utheemu unveils the historic residence known as Utheemu Ganduvaru, the childhood home of Sultan Mohamed Thakurufaanu, a national hero renowned for resisting Portuguese colonization in the 16th century. Preserving the architecture and artifacts of that era, this residence provides a glimpse into the Maldives' valiant history.

Maldives Maritime Museum
Nestled in Malé, the Maldives Maritime Museum pays homage to the nation's seafaring legacy. The exhibits showcase traditional fishing tools, navigational instruments, and models of historic vessels, offering an insight into the intimate relationship the Maldivian people share with the vast Indian Ocean.

Fua Mulaku Havitta
On the island of Fuvahmulah, the Fua Mulaku Havitta stands as an archaeological site shrouded in mystery. Believed to be a Buddhist stupa, this historical landmark

raises questions about the early cultural influences that touched the Maldives. The site serves as a reminder of the archipelago's connection to broader cultural and historical currents.

Medhu Ziyaaraiy: The Mysterious Tomb
Located on the island of Meedhoo in Addu Atoll, Medhu Ziyaaraiy is a sacred tomb shrouded in historical mystique. The tomb is believed to be the final resting place of a saint, and its serene surroundings invite reflection and contemplation.

The historical landmarks and museums in the Maldives present a kaleidoscope of cultural treasures, each telling a unique story of the nation's past. As you explore these sites, you embark on a journey that unravels the layers of Maldivian history, from the resilient narratives of ancient rulers to the contemporary expressions of a nation proud of its heritage. These landmarks stand not merely as remnants of the past but as living testaments to the enduring spirit that has shaped the Maldives into the enchanting archipelago it is today.

CHAPTER 4
Unveiling Maldives' Natural Wonders

In the heart of the Maldives lies a captivating chapter that unveils the enchanting tapestry of natural wonders. From pristine beaches that kiss the turquoise waters to vibrant coral reefs teeming with marine life, this exploration is an invitation to discover the awe-inspiring beauty that makes the Maldives a haven of unparalleled natural splendor.

Pristine Beaches and Islands

Must-Visit Beaches

Embark on a journey with us as we unravel the allure of the must-visit beaches in the Maldives, where the sun-kissed shores and crystalline waters paint a canvas of tranquility and natural splendor. Each beach, with its own unique charm, invites visitors into a realm of serenity and beauty that defines the quintessential Maldivian experience.

1. Veligandu Island Beach

Nestled in the North Ari Atoll, Veligandu Island Beach captivates with its powdery white sands and clear azure waters. The shallow lagoon surrounding the island creates a haven for snorkeling enthusiasts, offering glimpses of vibrant coral gardens and diverse marine life.

2. Bikini Beach, Rasdhoo
For those seeking a more secluded escape, Bikini Beach on Rasdhoo Island provides an intimate setting. With its soft sands and swaying palm trees, this beach is an idyllic retreat for relaxation, where visitors can bask in the gentle embrace of the Maldivian sun.

3. Fulhadhoo Beach
Fulhadhoo Island unveils a pristine stretch of beach untouched by time. Known for its tranquility, Fulhadhoo Beach is a sanctuary for those seeking solitude amid nature's beauty. The turquoise waters and coral-strewn shores create a mesmerizing panorama.

4. Hanifaru Bay Beach
Hanifaru Bay, located in the Baa Atoll, is not just a beach but a marine wonderland. Renowned as a UNESCO Biosphere Reserve, this beach offers a unique experience for snorkelers and divers alike, with the chance to witness majestic manta rays and whale sharks during the right seasons.

5. Ukulhas Bikini Beach
Ukulhas Island boasts a Bikini Beach that showcases the harmonious coexistence of tourism and local culture. With its designated swim area and pristine sands, this beach reflects the Maldives' commitment to sustainable tourism while providing a serene atmosphere for visitors.

6. Kandima Maldives Beach

Kandima Island unfolds a vibrant and lively beach experience. Known for its water sports and recreational activities, the beach at Kandima Maldives is a playground for adventure seekers. The lively atmosphere is complemented by the stunning sunset views that grace the horizon.

7. Maafushi Island Beach

Maafushi Island introduces travelers to the local way of life, and its beach mirrors the authenticity of Maldivian culture. Here, visitors can interact with locals, savor traditional cuisine, and enjoy the simplicity of island living against the backdrop of the Indian Ocean.

8. Thulusdhoo Island Beach

Thulusdhoo Island, famed for its surf breaks, unfolds a beach experience for water sports enthusiasts. The rhythmic waves beckon surfers, while the sandy shores provide a picturesque setting for leisurely strolls and unwinding beneath the tropical sun.

The must-visit beaches in the Maldives transcend mere landscapes; they embody the spirit of a tropical paradise where nature's beauty meets the warm embrace of island hospitality. Whether seeking solitude, adventure, or cultural immersion, each beach beckons with a promise of a unique and unforgettable Maldivian experience.

Hidden Islands to Explore
Embark on a captivating exploration of the Maldives as we uncover the hidden islands that add a touch of mystery to this tropical paradise. Beyond the well-trodden paths lies a tapestry of secluded atolls, each with its own unique charm and a promise of uncharted beauty waiting to be discovered.

1. Dhigurah Island
Nestled in the South Ari Atoll, Dhigurah Island unfolds as a hidden gem, celebrated for its long sandy stretches and vibrant local culture. Beyond its idyllic beaches, this island offers a glimpse into the authentic Maldivian way of life, where traditional craftsmanship and warm hospitality thrive.

2. Thoddoo Island
Thoddoo, situated in the Alif Alif Atoll, beckons travelers with its lush landscapes and expansive agricultural fields. Renowned as the 'breadbasket' of the Maldives, Thoddoo is a hidden haven for those seeking a tranquil retreat amidst swaying palms and the fragrance of tropical fruit orchards.

3. Mathiveri Island
Mathiveri, a tranquil island in the North Ari Atoll, unveils a harmonious blend of local life and untouched nature. Its coral-strewn shores and vibrant coral gardens make it a haven for snorkelers, while the winding pathways offer an opportunity to explore the island's hidden corners.

4. Thulusdhoo Island

Known as the 'Island of the Tuna, Thulusdhoo, located in the North Malé Atoll, is a hidden retreat for surf enthusiasts. Beyond its fame as a surfing destination, Thulusdhoo invites exploration of its traditional art scene, with local craftsmen renowned for their intricate skills in creating Maldivian crafts.

5. Gan Island

In the southernmost Addu Atoll, Gan Island stands as an undiscovered paradise with a rich history. Home to the largest Buddhist stupa in the Maldives, the island unfolds layers of cultural heritage waiting to be explored. Gan offers a unique blend of tranquility and historical significance.

6. Dhangethi Island

Dhangethi, located in the South Ari Atoll, reveals a hidden world beneath its waters. This island is a gateway to the famous Whale Shark Point, where lucky visitors can encounter these gentle giants in their natural habitat. Dhangethi provides an authentic Maldivian experience away from the bustling tourist hubs.

7. Fehendhoo Island

Fehendhoo, part of the Baa Atoll, is a testament to the Maldives' commitment to sustainable tourism. With its eco-friendly initiatives and pristine landscapes, Fehendhoo offers a secluded escape for nature lovers, where untouched beauty and responsible tourism go hand in hand.

8. Hulhudhoo Island
Tucked away in the Gaafu Alifu Atoll, Hulhudhoo Island offers a tranquil retreat for those seeking solitude. Known for its traditional coral stone houses and secluded beaches, Hulhudhoo provides a glimpse into the slower pace of island life away from the tourist crowds.

The hidden islands of the Maldives invite intrepid travelers to venture beyond the well-known atolls, unveiling a tapestry of natural beauty, cultural richness, and unexplored wonders. Each hidden island narrates its own story, and as you traverse these off-the-beaten-path destinations, you become part of the narrative, discovering the true essence of the Maldives.

Snorkeling and Diving Spots
Embark on an underwater odyssey as we delve into the mesmerizing world of snorkeling and diving spots in the Maldives. This tropical paradise, renowned for its crystal-clear waters and vibrant marine life, offers enthusiasts a plethora of sites to explore beneath the surface, each unveiling a unique marine ecosystem.

1. Maaya Thila
Located in the North Ari Atoll, Maaya Thila is a submerged pinnacle celebrated for its diverse marine life.

As snorkelers and divers descend into the depths, they encounter swirling schools of fish, colorful coral formations, and the possibility of encountering reef sharks and rays.

2. Banana Reef
In the North Malé Atoll, Banana Reef stands as one of the Maldives' most iconic dive sites. Shaped like a banana, this reef is adorned with intricate coral formations and a kaleidoscope of marine creatures. Snorkelers and divers alike are treated to the spectacle of vibrant fish darting through the underwater landscape.

3. Fish Head
Fish Head, located in the North Ari Atoll, is a renowned pinnacle dive site that captivates with its bustling marine activity. This underwater haven teems with schools of fish, including snappers and barracudas, creating a dynamic and visually stunning backdrop for diving enthusiasts.

4. Kuredu Express
For those seeking an exhilarating drift dive, Kuredu Express in the Lhaviyani Atoll offers an underwater adventure. The strong currents here attract pelagic species, making it a hotspot for witnessing sharks, rays, and other larger marine creatures cruising through the open ocean.

5. Manta Point
Situated in the South Ari Atoll, Manta Point lives up to its name as a gathering place for majestic manta rays. Snorkelers and divers are treated to close encounters with these graceful creatures as they glide through the water, creating an awe-inspiring spectacle.

6. HP Reef
In the North Malé Atoll, HP Reef enchants divers with its intricate coral formations and vibrant marine life. The reef's diverse topography, including overhangs and coral-covered walls, provides a canvas for a rich tapestry of marine species, from tiny reef fish to larger pelagic inhabitants.

7. Velassaru Caves
For a unique diving experience, Velassaru Caves in the South Malé Atoll beckon adventurers into a world of submerged caverns and swim-throughs. The play of light and shadow in these underwater caves creates an ethereal ambiance for divers exploring the hidden corners of the ocean.

8. Fotteyo Kandu
Fotteyo Kandu, located in the Felidhoo Atoll, is a channel dive known for its vibrant coral gardens and encounters with schools of fish. The channel's topography, with its overhangs and coral ridges, offers divers an opportunity to witness the dynamic marine life that thrives in this underwater highway.

The snorkeling and diving spots of the Maldives are a testament to the diversity and richness of the underwater world. Whether you are a novice snorkeler or an experienced diver, each site presents an opportunity to witness the beauty and biodiversity that make the Maldives a top destination for underwater enthusiasts. Dive into these azure waters, where every reef and pinnacle tells a story of the ocean's wonders waiting to be explored.

Marine Life Encounters

Best Places for Shark Watching

Embark on an awe-inspiring journey into the world of shark watching in the Maldives, where the vast azure waters play host to an impressive array of shark species. These magnificent creatures, rulers of the ocean, can be observed in their natural habitat, creating an unforgettable experience for enthusiasts seeking encounters with these apex predators.

1. South Ari Atoll

Renowned as a hotspot for whale shark sightings, the South Ari Atoll offers a unique opportunity for shark enthusiasts. The region's warm, nutrient-rich waters attract these gentle giants, providing snorkelers and divers a chance to witness the largest fish in the ocean gracefully swimming through the depths.

2. Fuvahmulah Atoll

Fuvahmulah, a unique atoll with a distinctive single island, is surrounded by deep channels. These channels attract various shark species, including reef sharks and hammerheads. The island's strategic location makes it an ideal destination for those seeking diverse shark encounters in the open ocean.

3. Vaavu Atoll

Vaavu Atoll, known for its vibrant coral reefs, also boasts excellent opportunities for shark watching. The atoll's channels and reef systems attract various shark species, including gray reef sharks and whitetip reef sharks. Divers can explore the underwater landscape while observing these fascinating creatures in their natural habitat.

4. Rasdhoo Atoll

Rasdhoo Atoll, situated in the heart of the Maldives, is a haven for shark enthusiasts. The atoll's diverse marine ecosystem is home to various shark species, including hammerheads and leopard sharks. Divers can explore the atoll's channels and vibrant coral formations while encountering these graceful predators.

5. Hanifaru Bay

While primarily famous for manta ray congregations, Hanifaru Bay in the Baa Atoll also offers opportunities for shark watching. The bay's nutrient-rich waters attract various shark species, creating a dynamic marine environment. Snorkelers can witness the coexistence of mantas and sharks in this unique setting.

6. Lhaviyani Atoll

Lhaviyani Atoll, known for its pristine coral reefs, is another gem for shark enthusiasts. The atoll's channels and vibrant underwater landscapes provide ideal conditions for encountering various shark species. Divers can explore the atoll's marine ecosystems while enjoying close encounters with these majestic predators.

7. Thaa Atoll

Thaa Atoll, a secluded paradise in the southern reaches of the Maldives, offers a tranquil setting for shark watching. The atoll's channels and coral gardens are frequented by different shark species, providing a serene and intimate experience for those seeking encounters with these fascinating creatures.

The Maldives stands as a premier destination for shark watching, offering diverse opportunities to observe these magnificent predators in their natural habitat. Whether in the channels, coral reefs, or open ocean expanses, each atoll presents a unique tapestry of marine life, making the Maldives a captivating haven for shark enthusiasts and nature lovers alike.

Coral Reefs and Vibrant Fish

Embark on a captivating journey beneath the waves as we explore the enchanting world of coral reefs and vibrant fish in the Maldives. The archipelago's warm, crystal-clear waters host a kaleidoscope of marine life, creating a mesmerizing tapestry of colors and biodiversity beneath the ocean's surface.

Coral reefs serve as the lifeblood of the marine ecosystem in the Maldives. These intricate structures, built by tiny coral polyps over centuries, provide a habitat for a diverse array of marine species. The Maldives is home to a variety of coral reef types, from fringing reefs that hug the shores of islands to barrier reefs that form offshore, creating a dynamic underwater landscape.

As sunlight penetrates the pristine waters of the Maldives, it breathes life into the coral reefs, initiating a process called photosynthesis. Coral polyps, which have a symbiotic relationship with algae known as zooxanthellae, harness the energy from sunlight to create food. This interaction not only sustains the corals but also contributes to the vibrant colors that adorn the reefs.

The coral reefs of the Maldives are a haven for an astonishing variety of fish species. From the flamboyant parrotfish to the sleek and agile surgeonfish, these underwater wonders create a mesmerizing spectacle for snorkelers and divers. The reefs teem with life as schools of colorful fish weave through the corals, creating a dynamic and lively underwater panorama.

Among the myriad fish species, the Maldives is also renowned for its charismatic megafauna. Majestic manta rays gracefully glide through the water, their wings spanning in elegant arcs. Whale sharks, the largest fish in the ocean, make seasonal appearances, offering divers and snorkelers the opportunity for awe-inspiring encounters.

The biodiversity of the Maldivian coral reefs extends beyond fish to include an array of invertebrates. Delicate sea anemones sway in the currents, providing shelter for clownfish. Elegant seahorses grasp onto corals with their prehensile tails, camouflaging seamlessly with their surroundings.

The coral reefs not only serve as a visual spectacle but also play a crucial role in maintaining the balance of the marine ecosystem. They provide a habitat for countless marine organisms, support local fisheries, and act as natural barriers, protecting the islands from the erosive forces of the ocean.

However, these fragile ecosystems face threats from climate change, coral bleaching, and human activities. Conservation efforts in the Maldives aim to protect and preserve these invaluable reefs for future generations, emphasizing the importance of sustainable tourism and responsible environmental practices.

In conclusion, the coral reefs and vibrant fish of the Maldives weave a tale of natural splendor beneath the ocean's surface. As guardians of this delicate ecosystem, it is our collective responsibility to appreciate, protect, and ensure the longevity of these underwater wonders, allowing the beauty of the Maldivian marine world to thrive for generations to come.

Dolphin and Whale Watching
Embark on an extraordinary oceanic adventure as we delve into the captivating world of dolphin and whale watching in the Maldives. The azure waters surrounding the archipelago provide a playground for these majestic marine mammals, offering an enchanting experience for wildlife enthusiasts and nature lovers alike.

Dolphin Watching
The Maldives is renowned for its thriving populations of playful dolphins, including the charismatic spinner dolphins and the acrobatic bottlenose dolphins. These sociable creatures are often spotted riding the bow waves of boats, leaping and somersaulting in a joyful display. The atolls and channels of the Maldives serve as prime locations for dolphin encounters, creating a magical connection between humans and these highly intelligent beings.

Dolphin watching excursions typically take place during calm mornings or at sunset when these marine acrobats are most active. As the boat glides through the tranquil waters, the sight of dolphins frolicking in the ocean creates a sense of awe and wonder. Sunset dolphin cruises, in particular, offer a surreal backdrop as the sky transforms into a canvas of warm hues, complementing the playful antics of the dolphins.

Whale Watching
Beyond dolphins, the Maldives also hosts an array of whale species, making it a hotspot for whale watching enthusiasts. The deep channels surrounding the atolls attract different whale species, including the awe-inspiring blue whales, the largest animals on Earth. Other species like pilot whales, sperm whales, and even the elusive orcas are also occasional visitors to the Maldivian waters.

Whale watching excursions involve venturing into the open ocean, guided by experienced naturalists who are well-versed in the behavior and migratory patterns of these magnificent creatures. The vast expanse of the ocean becomes a stage for witnessing these giants breaching, tail-slapping, and gracefully navigating the waters. The thrill of encountering a whale in its natural habitat leaves an indelible impression, fostering a deep appreciation for marine conservation.

Ethical Practices

In the Maldives, responsible and ethical practices are emphasized in both dolphin and whale watching experiences. Operators adhere to guidelines that prioritize the well-being of the animals, maintaining a respectful distance to avoid disturbance. The focus is on creating educational and sustainable encounters that contribute to the conservation efforts for these marine species.

Conservation Awareness

Dolphin and whale watching excursions in the Maldives not only provide an exhilarating experience but also serve as platforms for raising awareness about marine conservation. Guided by marine biologists and naturalists, participants gain insights into the importance of protecting these marine ecosystems and the need for sustainable tourism practices to ensure the well-being of these incredible creatures.

The Maldives offers a front-row seat to the enchanting world of dolphin and whale watching, where every excursion becomes a unique and awe-inspiring journey into the heart of the ocean. As we witness these marine wonders in their natural habitat, the experience becomes a poignant reminder of the need to cherish, protect, and conserve the rich biodiversity that thrives beneath the surface of the Maldivian waters.

Chapter 5
Activities for Different Traveler Types

Embark on a journey that caters to every kind of traveler. Whether you're exploring solo, savoring moments as a couple, creating family memories, or relishing the camaraderie of friends, this chapter unveils a spectrum of activities designed just for you.

Solo Traveler's Guide

Solo-Friendly Activities
Embark on a solo odyssey in the Maldives, where the beauty of this tropical paradise unfolds uniquely for the lone explorer. Whether you seek tranquility or adventure, the archipelago offers a spectrum of solo-friendly activities that embrace the spirit of solo travel.

Exploring Island Culture
Immerse yourself in the rich Maldivian culture by exploring local islands. Wander through vibrant markets, engage with friendly locals, and witness traditional ceremonies. This solo adventure allows you to delve into the heart of Maldivian life, fostering a deeper connection with the destination.

Underwater Exploration
For solo adventurers seeking solitude beneath the waves, the Maldives' renowned dive sites beckon. Dive into the crystal-clear waters to discover vibrant coral reefs teeming with marine life. Solo diving allows for a more intimate connection with the underwater world, where every fin movement unveils a new facet of the mesmerizing marine ecosystem.

Wellness Retreats
Indulge in self-discovery and rejuvenation at the Maldives' world-class wellness retreats. Solo travelers can partake in yoga sessions by the beach, spa treatments overlooking the ocean, and mindfulness activities that harmonize with the serenity of the surroundings. These retreats provide a sanctuary for solitary reflection and personal renewal.

Sunset Cruises
Set sail on a solo sunset cruise, where the changing hues of the sky mirror the tranquility within. Private boat charters offer a peaceful journey across the azure waters, allowing solo travelers to bask in the breathtaking beauty of a Maldivian sunset without the distractions of a crowd.

Culinary Adventures
Solo dining becomes a culinary exploration in the Maldives. Relish the flavors of Maldivian cuisine in beachfront restaurants or opt for private dining experiences under the starlit sky. This gastronomic journey provides

solo travelers with an opportunity to savor the local tastes while enjoying the solitude of their own company.

Nature Walks and Bird Watching
Embark on solo nature walks through the lush landscapes of uninhabited islands. The Maldives' biodiversity, including rare bird species, awaits discovery. Binoculars in hand, solo travelers can wander through the island's trails, connecting with nature and encountering unique flora and fauna along the way.

Photography Expeditions
For solo adventurers with a passion for photography, the Maldives becomes a canvas of captivating moments. Capture the essence of island life, the vivid marine life, and the scenic landscapes with a camera in hand. Solo photography expeditions allow for creative exploration and the crafting of a personal visual narrative.

Solo travel in the Maldives transcends the conventional, offering a bespoke experience tailored to the preferences of the individual explorer. Whether seeking solitude or engaging in thrilling adventures, the Maldives unfolds its treasures uniquely for those who embark on the solo journey, ensuring an enriching and self-reflective exploration of this idyllic destination.

Safety Tips

Embarking on a solo journey in the Maldives is an exhilarating adventure, and ensuring your safety is paramount. Here, we delve into essential safety tips crafted to make your solo sojourn a secure and worry-free experience.

Understanding Local Customs and Laws

Before you set foot on this tropical paradise, take a moment to familiarize yourself with the local customs and laws. Respecting the cultural nuances of the Maldives fosters a harmonious environment and ensures that your interactions with locals are positive and respectful.

Accommodation Choice

Opt for accommodations that prioritize safety. Reputable guesthouses, resorts, and hotels often implement stringent security measures to guarantee the well-being of their guests. Check reviews and choose establishments with a track record of providing a secure environment for solo travelers.

Communication and Connectivity

Ensure you have reliable means of communication during your solo journey. Local SIM cards or international roaming services can keep you connected, allowing you to reach out for assistance or share your experiences with loved ones. Familiarize yourself with emergency contact numbers and the location of the nearest embassy.

Informed Itinerary Planning
While spontaneity adds flavor to solo travel, having a rough itinerary in place enhances your safety. Share your planned activities and whereabouts with someone you trust. This ensures that, in the event of unforeseen circumstances, someone knows your general location and can offer assistance if needed.

Health and Medical Precautions
Prioritize your health by taking necessary precautions. Ensure you have access to a basic first aid kit and any essential medications you may need. Familiarize yourself with the location of medical facilities on the islands you plan to visit, and carry a copy of your medical information, including any allergies or existing conditions.

Safe Exploration
Explore with confidence by choosing well-traveled routes and avoiding isolated areas, especially after dark. While the Maldives is generally safe, it's prudent to exercise caution in unfamiliar surroundings. Trust your instincts, and if something feels off, opt for a more populated and well-lit route.

Responsible Alcohol Consumption
If you choose to indulge in the vibrant nightlife the Maldives has to offer, do so responsibly. Excessive alcohol consumption can impair judgment and leave you vulnerable. Stay within your limits, and be mindful of your

surroundings, particularly when in unfamiliar areas or social settings.

Secure Valuables
Keep your belongings secure by utilizing hotel safes and being mindful of your possessions in public spaces. Consider carrying a photocopy of important documents and leaving the originals in a secure location. This ensures that, in the unfortunate event of loss, you have a backup.

Local Guidance and Recommendations
Tap into the wealth of local knowledge by seeking guidance from residents or your accommodation hosts. Locals can provide insights into safe areas, cultural nuances, and hidden gems worth exploring. Their advice can enhance your experience while keeping you informed about potential safety considerations.

Solo travel in the Maldives can be a fulfilling and secure adventure with a mindful approach to safety. By understanding local customs, choosing secure accommodations, maintaining communication, and adopting responsible practices, you can savor every moment of your solo sojourn while prioritizing your well-being.

Meeting Other Travellers
Embarking on a solo adventure in the Maldives doesn't mean journeying alone; rather, it opens the door to a world

of opportunities for meeting fellow travelers. The archipelago, with its inviting atmosphere, creates a conducive environment for solo explorers to connect, share experiences, and forge new friendships along the way.

Common Spaces in Accommodations
Many accommodations in the Maldives feature communal spaces where solo travelers naturally gravitate. Shared lounges, dining areas, and recreational zones become hubs for chance encounters. Engaging in casual conversations over a cup of coffee or a meal can be the gateway to meeting like-minded individuals from various corners of the globe.

Excursions and Group Activities
Participating in group excursions and activities tailored for solo travelers provides a structured yet enjoyable way to meet others. Whether it's a snorkeling trip, island hopping, or a guided nature walk, these shared experiences create opportunities for spontaneous interactions and the formation of travel companionships.

Social Events and Gatherings
Resorts and guesthouses often organize social events, creating a vibrant platform for solo travelers to mingle. Beach barbecues, cultural nights, or sunset gatherings offer relaxed settings where conversations flow naturally. These events provide a delightful backdrop for forging

connections amidst the beauty of the Maldivian surroundings.

Online Travel Communities
In the digital age, solo travelers can leverage online platforms and travel communities to connect with others planning trips to the Maldives. Forums, social media groups, and travel apps enable individuals to share plans, seek advice, and even arrange meet-ups with fellow adventurers, turning virtual connections into real-life friendships.

Engaging with Locals
The warmth of Maldivian hospitality extends to interactions with the locals. Solo travelers can engage in conversations with island residents, gaining insights into local culture and traditions. These genuine exchanges often lead to unexpected friendships, offering a deeper understanding of the Maldives beyond its picturesque landscapes.

Cultural Workshops and Classes
Participating in cultural workshops or classes becomes a dual experience, allowing solo travelers not only to learn a new skill or craft but also to interact with fellow learners. Whether it's a traditional Maldivian cooking class or a handicraft workshop, these activities foster camaraderie among participants.

Solo Traveler Meet-Up Events
Some accommodations and travel agencies host solo traveler meet-up events specifically designed to bring individuals together. These events, ranging from casual mixers to organized dinners, create a friendly atmosphere for solo adventurers to share stories, exchange tips, and potentially form travel companionships for various activities.

Solo travel in the Maldives unveils a myriad of avenues for connecting with other travelers. Whether through shared spaces in accommodations, group activities, online communities, or cultural engagements, the solo explorer discovers that the journey is not just about the destination but also about the connections made along the way. The Maldives, with its inviting spirit, becomes a canvas for weaving a tapestry of shared experiences and newfound friendships.

Couples Retreat

Romantic Dinner Spots
Embark on a journey to discover the enchanting romantic dinner spots scattered across the idyllic islands of the Maldives. These exquisite locations not only offer delectable culinary experiences but also create an intimate ambiance, making them perfect settings for couples seeking a memorable evening in this tropical paradise.

Overwater Dining

Indulge in the epitome of romance with overwater dining experiences. Many resorts in the Maldives feature private overwater bungalows or decks where couples can relish a candlelit dinner with the gentle lull of the ocean beneath. The unobstructed views of the starlit sky and surrounding turquoise waters provide an enchanting backdrop for a romantic rendezvous.

Beachfront Elegance

Feel the softness of white sand beneath your feet as you enjoy a romantic dinner on the pristine beaches of the Maldives. Many resorts offer beachfront dining setups, allowing couples to savor a delectable meal while listening to the rhythmic sounds of the waves and feeling the gentle caress of the ocean breeze.

Underwater Marvels

For a truly unique and immersive dining experience, some resorts in the Maldives offer underwater restaurants. Imagine being surrounded by the mesmerizing aquatic world as you share a meal with your loved one. These underwater dining spots provide a surreal setting, allowing couples to enjoy each other's company while surrounded by vibrant marine life.

Private Sunset Cruises

Embark on a private sunset cruise for an intimate dining experience on the waters of the Maldives. Drift away with your significant other as the sun paints the sky in hues of pink and orange. Many cruises include a specially curated dinner, offering couples a secluded and romantic setting amidst the vastness of the Indian Ocean.

Dining Under the Stars
Revel in the celestial beauty of the Maldivian night sky with a dining experience under the stars. Resorts often set up private dining areas on open-air terraces or decks, allowing couples to dine beneath a blanket of stars. The soft glow of candlelight adds a touch of magic to the evening, creating a romantic atmosphere.

Island Hideaways
Escape to a secluded island for a private and intimate dinner. Some resorts offer the option to arrange a romantic meal on a deserted island, providing couples with the ultimate privacy and seclusion. Surrounded by nature and the sounds of the ocean, it's a perfect setting for a romantic celebration.

Culinary Extravaganza
Discover the diverse culinary offerings of the Maldives with a romantic dinner that showcases the best of local and international cuisines. Many resorts feature specialty restaurants where couples can enjoy a curated menu, expertly crafted to tantalize the taste buds in a romantic and elegant setting.

In summary, the Maldives presents a tapestry of romantic dinner spots, each offering a unique and unforgettable experience. Whether it's the overwater allure, beachfront serenity, underwater enchantment, or celestial dining, couples can find the perfect setting to celebrate love amidst the breathtaking beauty of the Maldivian islands.

Private Island Escapes
Embark on a journey of tranquility and seclusion with private island escapes in the Maldives, where the essence of exclusivity merges with the pristine beauty of nature. These secluded paradises offer a haven for those seeking a retreat from the ordinary, providing an intimate and personalized experience amidst the turquoise waters and lush landscapes of the Maldivian archipelago.

Island Resorts
Several luxury resorts in the Maldives boast private island accommodations, providing guests with the ultimate escape. These exclusive retreats often feature standalone villas or bungalows surrounded by expansive gardens, ensuring complete privacy and a sense of being in a world of your own.

Intimate Villas and Bungalows
Private island escapes offer a range of intimate villas and bungalows, each designed to provide seclusion and comfort. With direct access to pristine beaches or perched over crystal-clear waters, these accommodations create an

idyllic setting for couples, families, or solo travelers looking for a serene escape.

Personalized Service
The hallmark of private island escapes in the Maldives is the personalized service extended to guests. Dedicated staff members cater to every need, ensuring a seamless and tailored experience. From private butlers to personalized dining options, the emphasis is on creating a bespoke retreat that aligns with individual preferences.

Exclusive Dining Experiences
Indulge in culinary delights with exclusive dining experiences tailored to your preferences. Private island resorts often offer personalized menus, allowing guests to savor gourmet meals in intimate settings, whether it's a beachfront dinner under the stars or a private picnic on a secluded stretch of sand.

Secluded Beaches and Lagoons
One of the enchanting aspects of private island escapes is the access to secluded beaches and lagoons. Guests can bask in the sun on their private stretch of sand, take a dip in crystal-clear waters, or embark on snorkeling adventures in the privacy of their personal aquatic haven.

Wellness and Spa Retreats
Private island resorts frequently feature wellness and spa facilities, providing guests with rejuvenating experiences

surrounded by nature. From overwater spa pavilions to wellness retreats nestled in lush greenery, these sanctuaries offer a holistic approach to relaxation and rejuvenation.

Water Villas with Panoramic Views
For those seeking an elevated experience, private island escapes often include luxurious water villas with panoramic views of the surrounding ocean. These overwater retreats offer a heightened sense of seclusion, allowing guests to immerse themselves in the breathtaking beauty of the Maldivian seascape.

Tailored Activities and Excursions
Guests at private island resorts can tailor their Maldivian experience with a variety of activities and excursions. Whether it's a private dolphin cruise, a guided snorkeling expedition, or a sunset yacht excursion, the possibilities are curated to individual preferences, ensuring a personalized and unforgettable stay.

Private island escapes in the Maldives offer a symphony of exclusivity, personalized service, and natural beauty. These secluded havens cater to the desire for tranquility, providing a respite from the hustle and bustle of daily life. Whether seeking a romantic retreat or a peaceful family getaway, the Maldives' private islands beckon with the promise of an extraordinary and tailor-made experience.

Family Adventures

Kid-Friendly Attractions

Discovering the Maldives with your little ones is a delightful adventure, as this tropical paradise offers a range of kid-friendly attractions that cater to the curiosity and wonder of young explorers. From vibrant marine life to exciting water activities, the Maldives ensures that families create cherished memories in this breathtaking archipelago.

Underwater Adventures

One of the most captivating experiences for children in the Maldives is the underwater world teeming with colorful marine life. Many resorts offer snorkeling excursions suitable for kids, allowing them to marvel at the kaleidoscope of fish and coral formations in the clear turquoise waters.

Family-Friendly Resorts

Several resorts in the Maldives go the extra mile to cater to families by providing kid-friendly amenities and activities. These family-centric resorts often feature dedicated kids' clubs, where little ones can engage in supervised games, crafts, and educational activities, ensuring both entertainment and enrichment.

Educational Marine Centers

For young marine enthusiasts, the Maldives hosts educational marine centers that offer insights into the unique oceanic ecosystem. These centers often feature interactive exhibits, allowing children to learn about marine conservation and the diverse species that call the Maldives home.

Dolphin Watching Excursions
Embark on exciting dolphin-watching excursions with your family to witness these playful creatures in their natural habitat. The Maldives' warm waters are home to various dolphin species, and children can marvel at their acrobatic displays as they frolic in the Indian Ocean.

Water Sports for Kids
Introduce your little adventurers to the thrill of water sports tailored for their age and skill levels. Resorts often offer activities such as paddleboarding, kayaking, and banana boat rides, providing children with a safe and enjoyable introduction to the wonders of the ocean.

Sandbank Picnics
Create lasting family memories with sandbank picnics, where you can enjoy a delightful meal on a secluded sandbank surrounded by the turquoise ocean. This idyllic setting allows children to play in the soft sand and explore the natural beauty of their surroundings.

Cultural Excursions
Immerse your family in the rich cultural heritage of the Maldives through guided excursions to local islands. Children can discover traditional Maldivian customs,

explore vibrant markets, and interact with friendly locals, providing them with a broader cultural perspective.

Resort-Organized Activities
Many resorts organize a variety of kid-friendly activities, from treasure hunts to arts and crafts sessions. These activities are designed to entertain and engage young minds while allowing parents to relax and enjoy their vacation.

Safe Snorkeling Areas
Opt for family-friendly snorkeling spots that offer calm and shallow waters, ensuring a safe and enjoyable experience for children. Resorts often designate specific areas suitable for families, allowing kids to marvel at the underwater wonders with ease.

The Maldives welcomes families with open arms, providing a diverse array of kid-friendly attractions and activities. From educational marine experiences to exciting water adventures, this enchanting destination ensures that children and parents alike create magical moments together in the heart of the Indian Ocean.

Family-Focused Excursions
In the heart of the Indian Ocean, the Maldives beckons families to embark on a series of family-focused excursions, each promising unforgettable moments amidst the archipelago's turquoise waters and pristine landscapes. Tailored to cater to all ages, these excursions provide a

perfect blend of adventure, education, and relaxation for families seeking to create cherished memories together.

Island-Hopping Adventures
Embark on island-hopping escapades to explore the diverse beauty of the Maldives. Guided by knowledgeable locals, families can visit different islands, each offering a unique glimpse into Maldivian culture, traditions, and local life. From bustling markets to serene fishing villages, these excursions provide a captivating experience for both parents and children.

Snorkeling Safaris
Delve into the underwater wonders of the Maldives with family-friendly snorkeling safaris. Guided by experienced instructors, these excursions take families to vibrant coral reefs teeming with a kaleidoscope of marine life. Children and adults alike can marvel at the colorful fish, gentle rays, and maybe even spot a friendly sea turtle or two.

Dolphin Cruises
Set sail on family-friendly dolphin cruises to witness the playful antics of these charismatic marine creatures. The Maldives is home to various dolphin species, and these excursions offer a chance to see them leaping and dancing in the wake of the boat. It's an enchanting experience that captures the imagination of young and old alike.

Picnic on Sandbanks
Create lasting family memories with picnics on secluded sandbanks surrounded by the azure waters of the Indian Ocean. These excursions provide a private and idyllic setting where families can relax, play in the soft sand, and savor a delicious meal prepared by the resort. It's a perfect blend of tranquility and togetherness.

Cultural Village Tours
Immerse your family in the rich cultural heritage of the Maldives with guided tours to local villages. These excursions offer insights into traditional Maldivian life, allowing children to witness age-old customs, explore vibrant markets, and interact with friendly locals. It's a cultural journey that broadens perspectives and fosters understanding.

Fishing Adventures
For families with budding anglers, fishing excursions in the Maldives provide an exciting opportunity to try traditional line fishing or even night fishing under the starlit sky. Local guides share their expertise, ensuring an enjoyable and educational experience for all family members.

Water Sports Extravaganza
Indulge in a water sports extravaganza designed for families. From banana boat rides to kayaking and paddleboarding, these excursions cater to various skill levels and ages. Resorts often organize these activities,

allowing families to bond over thrilling water adventures in a safe and supervised environment.

Maldivian Sunset Cruise
End your day with a breathtaking Maldivian sunset cruise. Aboard a traditional dhoni, families can relax and soak in the golden hues of the setting sun over the Indian Ocean. It's a serene and magical experience that adds a touch of romance to family-focused excursions.

Family-focused excursions in the Maldives offer a tapestry of experiences that cater to the diverse interests of family members. From cultural explorations to underwater adventures, these excursions weave together the fabric of togetherness, ensuring that families leave the Maldives with hearts full of shared memories and the desire to return to this tropical paradise.

Educational Activities for Children
In the sun-kissed embrace of the Maldives, a world of educational wonders awaits children, blending fun and learning seamlessly against the backdrop of turquoise waters and sandy shores. The Maldives, known for its breathtaking beauty, also offers a treasure trove of educational activities that captivate young minds and spark curiosity.

Marine Biology Workshops
For budding marine enthusiasts, the Maldives hosts engaging marine biology workshops. Led by knowledgeable experts, these workshops introduce children to the fascinating world beneath the waves. Kids can learn about colorful coral reefs, diverse marine species, and the importance of ocean conservation in an interactive and enjoyable environment.

Seaside Storytelling Sessions
Under the shade of palm trees, seaside storytelling sessions transport children to magical worlds through captivating tales. Storytellers weave narratives inspired by Maldivian folklore and marine adventures, fostering a love for storytelling and igniting the imagination of young listeners.

Coral Planting Initiatives
Environmental stewardship takes center stage with coral planting initiatives designed for children. In collaboration with marine conservation organizations, kids can actively participate in coral restoration efforts. These hands-on experiences not only educate them about the fragile ecosystem but also instill a sense of responsibility for the environment.

Traditional Maldivian Craft Workshops
Immerse children in the rich cultural heritage of the Maldives through traditional craft workshops. Guided by local artisans, kids can create their own dhonis (traditional

Maldivian boats), learn intricate hand-weaving techniques, or try their hand at crafting vibrant traditional garlands.

Underwater Classroom Excursions
Transforming the ocean into a classroom, underwater excursions with educational guides provide a unique opportunity for children to explore the marine world up close. Equipped with snorkeling gear, kids can witness the vibrant coral gardens and interact with marine life while gaining insights into the importance of preserving the delicate balance of the underwater ecosystem.

Astronomy Nights on the Beach
Gaze at the star-studded Maldivian night sky during astronomy nights on the beach. Led by astronomers or knowledgeable guides, children can marvel at constellations, learn about celestial bodies, and even spot the Milky Way. It's an enchanting blend of science and wonder against the backdrop of the serene Maldivian night.

Language and Cultural Lessons
Engage children in language and cultural lessons that offer a glimpse into the unique heritage of the Maldives. Interactive sessions can include learning Dhivehi phrases, discovering traditional Maldivian songs, and understanding the significance of cultural practices. These activities promote cultural appreciation and global awareness.

Guided Snorkeling with Marine Educators
Guided snorkeling excursions with marine educators provide an educational twist to underwater exploration. Children can snorkel alongside knowledgeable guides who share insights into the marine ecosystem, pointing out different species and explaining the interconnectedness of marine life.

Interactive Cooking Classes
Introduce children to the flavors of Maldivian cuisine through interactive cooking classes. Led by local chefs, these classes allow kids to participate in preparing simple Maldivian dishes, offering a hands-on experience that blends culinary skills with cultural awareness.

The educational activities for children in the Maldives weave together the threads of fun, curiosity, and learning, creating an enriching tapestry of experiences that linger in the hearts and minds of young adventurers. Amidst the stunning natural beauty of the Maldives, these activities nurture a lifelong love for exploration, education, and the wonders of the world.

CHAPTER 6
Essential Things to Pack

Embarking on your journey to the enchanting Maldives requires thoughtful preparation, and a crucial step in ensuring a smooth and enjoyable adventure is knowing what to pack. In this chapter, we'll guide you through the essential items to bring, ensuring you're well-equipped for the sun-soaked beaches, vibrant coral reefs, and cultural delights that await. Let's dive into the must-haves that will enhance your Maldivian experience, ensuring you make the most of every moment in this tropical paradise.

Clothing and Footwear

Packing Tips for the Maldives Climate

When preparing for your journey to the Maldives, understanding the unique climate of this tropical paradise is paramount to ensuring a comfortable and enjoyable stay. The Maldives experiences a distinct climatic pattern, characterized by two primary seasons: the dry northeast monsoon season (Iruvai) and the wet southwest monsoon season (Hulhangu).

Packing for the Dry Northeast Monsoon Season (Iruvai)
During the dry season from December to April, the Maldives enjoys clear skies, abundant sunshine, and calm seas. Here are some packing tips tailored to this period:

Light and Breathable Clothing

Given the predominantly sunny weather, pack lightweight and breathable clothing. Cotton and linen fabrics are excellent choices, allowing your skin to stay cool amidst the gentle tropical breeze.

Sun Protection Essentials

With the sun shining generously, include sun protection essentials such as sunscreen with a high SPF, sunglasses, and a wide-brimmed hat. These items safeguard you from the radiant tropical sun, ensuring your skin stays protected.

Swimwear and Beach Accessories

The dry season beckons beach exploration and water activities. Don't forget to pack your favorite swimwear, beach towels, and accessories like snorkeling gear for underwater adventures.

Casual and Elegant Attire

Evenings may bring a mild drop in temperature, so having a few casual-chic outfits for dinner or evening strolls is advisable. A light sweater or shawl can provide warmth during cooler nights.

Packing for the Wet Southwest Monsoon Season (Hulhangu)

From May to November, the wet season introduces occasional rain showers and stronger winds. Here's how to prepare for this period:

Waterproof Attire and Accessories

Given the likelihood of rain, pack waterproof items like a travel-sized umbrella, a lightweight rain jacket, and waterproof footwear. These items ensure you stay dry during brief tropical downpours.

Quick-Drying Clothing

Opt for quick-drying fabrics during the wet season. These materials allow you to easily manage any unexpected rain encounters and keep you comfortable as the humidity levels rise.

Mosquito Repellent

The wet season brings an increase in mosquito activity. Packing a reliable mosquito repellent helps ward off these tiny nuisances and ensures peaceful nights.

Comfortable Footwear

With occasional rain, consider sturdy yet breathable shoes that provide good traction. This ensures you can explore the islands without worrying about slippery surfaces.

Regardless of the season, a comprehensive packing strategy includes a mix of essentials to cater to both the sunny and rainy aspects of the Maldivian climate. By adapting your wardrobe to these climatic nuances, you're better equipped to make the most of your tropical getaway, come rain or shine.

Beachwear Essentials
Embarking on a sun-kissed sojourn to the Maldives calls for a well-curated collection of beachwear essentials. As the radiant sun dances upon the turquoise waters and pristine sands, embracing the laid-back charm of beach life becomes a delightful part of your Maldivian adventure.

Swimwear
At the heart of your beachwear ensemble lies the quintessential swimwear. Choose swim trunks, bikinis, or one-piece swimsuits that not only complement your style but also provide comfort for the myriad of water activities the Maldives offers. Vibrant colors and patterns resonate harmoniously with the vivid surroundings, adding a touch of tropical flair to your beach look.

Cover-ups
Transition seamlessly from beachside bliss to casual strolls with the inclusion of stylish cover-ups. Lightweight and airy, these garments offer a modicum of coverage while allowing the gentle ocean breeze to playfully caress your

skin. Flowing dresses, sarongs, or kaftans serve as versatile options, effortlessly elevating your beachwear style.

Sun Protection
Under the tropical sun, protection is paramount. Equip yourself with a wide-brimmed hat to shield your face from direct sunlight. Sunglasses not only add a dash of glamour but also safeguard your eyes from the radiant rays. Applying a high SPF sunscreen becomes a ritual, ensuring your skin remains shielded as you revel in the Maldivian sunshine.

Footwear
Embrace the laid-back island vibe with comfortable and practical footwear. Flip-flops or sandals are perfect companions for sandy strolls and beachside relaxation. For more adventurous pursuits like snorkeling or exploring coral reefs, consider water-friendly shoes that provide both protection and traction.

Beach Accessories
Enhance your beach experience with thoughtfully chosen accessories. A lightweight beach bag proves invaluable for carrying essentials like sunscreen, a good book, and a refreshing beverage. A beach towel, adorned with vibrant colors, becomes your cozy retreat for soaking in the sun or watching the gentle waves.

Casual Evening Attire

As the sun sets, transitioning seamlessly from the beach to evening activities calls for a touch of casual elegance. Pack a few casual-chic outfits for sunset dinners or beachside cocktails. A light sweater or shawl may come in handy as the night breeze brings a gentle coolness to the air.

Crafting your beachwear essentials for the Maldives is about blending comfort, style, and functionality. Embrace the island spirit with outfits that mirror the vibrant hues of the Maldivian landscape, allowing you to bask in the beauty of this tropical haven with effortless grace.

Snorkeling and Diving Gear

Embarking on the underwater wonders of the Maldives, whether through snorkeling or diving, requires thoughtful consideration of essential gear. Equipping yourself with the right tools ensures a seamless exploration of the vibrant marine life that graces the crystal-clear waters surrounding the Maldivian atolls.

Must-Have Equipment

1. Mask and Snorkel

A well-fitted mask and snorkel are fundamental for both snorkeling and diving adventures. The mask provides a clear view of the underwater world, while the snorkel enables effortless breathing at the water's surface.

2. Fins
Fins are your underwater propulsion system, allowing you to navigate the ocean currents with ease. Choose fins that offer comfort and a snug fit for optimal performance.

3. Wetsuit or Rash Guard
Depending on your preference and the water temperature, a wetsuit or rash guard provides thermal protection and shields your skin from potential irritants.

4. Dive Computer
For avid divers, a dive computer is an invaluable tool that tracks your depth, dive time, and decompression limits. It enhances safety and aids in planning subsequent dives.

5. Underwater Camera
Capture the mesmerizing underwater landscapes by bringing along a waterproof camera. Immortalize your encounters with colorful coral reefs and exotic marine life to share your Maldivian adventure.

Rental Options
For travelers looking to minimize baggage or those new to snorkeling and diving, many resorts and local dive shops in the Maldives offer rental services. Renting equipment provides a convenient and cost-effective solution, ensuring you have access to quality gear without the need for ownership.

Electronics and Gadgets

1. Waterproof Phone Case

Safeguard your smartphone from water exposure with a reliable waterproof case. This allows you to capture photos or videos while snorkeling and diving without worrying about potential damage.

2. Underwater Flashlight

Enhance your underwater visibility during dawn or dusk dives with an underwater flashlight. Illuminate the vibrant colors of coral formations and marine life hidden in the shadows.

3. Underwater Scooter

For an added thrill, consider renting an underwater scooter. This gadget propels you through the water, offering a unique and effortless way to explore the underwater realm.

Whether you're a seasoned diver or a novice snorkeler, the Maldives beckons with a breathtaking underwater panorama. Equipping yourself with the right gear ensures a safe and immersive experience, allowing you to delve into the enchanting world beneath the waves.

CHAPTER 7
Navigating Local Cuisine and Dining

Embarking on a culinary journey through the Maldives offers a delectable fusion of flavors that mirror the rich cultural tapestry of the islands. In this chapter, we explore the vibrant tapestry of local cuisine, guiding you through the diverse culinary landscape that awaits. From traditional Maldivian delicacies to international fare, get ready to savor the tastes that define the gastronomic charm of the Maldives. Join us as we navigate the intricacies of local dining, ensuring every bite is a memorable experience that captures the essence of these tropical isles.

Traditional Maldivian Dishes

Embarking on a culinary exploration of the Maldives unveils a treasure trove of traditional dishes that mirror the cultural heritage and local flavors of this tropical paradise. The Maldivian cuisine, deeply rooted in the archipelago's history, showcases a delightful array of dishes that tantalize the taste buds with their unique blends of spices, fresh ingredients, and aromatic nuances.

Garudhiya

One of the iconic dishes of the Maldives, Garudhiya, is a fish soup that embodies the essence of Maldivian coastal living. Prepared using tuna, coconut, chili, and lemon, this hearty soup is often accompanied by rice, lime, chili, and onions. It serves as a flavorful ode to the maritime traditions of the Maldivian people.

Mas Huni

A staple breakfast dish, Mas Huni, is a simple yet satisfying blend of tuna, coconut, onion, chili, and lime. This mixture is typically enjoyed with flatbread known as roshi. Mas Huni not only provides a nutritious start to the day but also offers a glimpse into the daily life of Maldivians.

Fihunu Mas

For those who relish grilled delights, Fihunu Mas, or grilled fish, is a culinary delight. Marinated in a blend of Maldivian spices and grilled to perfection, this dish showcases the Maldivian mastery of enhancing the natural flavors of seafood.

Banbukeylu Harissa

A dessert that delights the sweet tooth, Banbukeylu Harissa is a traditional Maldivian sweet made from bananas, coconut, and sugar. This delectable treat offers a perfect balance of sweetness and tropical richness, reflecting the abundance of natural ingredients in the Maldives.

Saagu Bondibai
Saagu Bondibai, a comforting dessert, features tapioca pearls cooked in coconut milk and sweetened with sugar. This dessert, often infused with cardamom for a fragrant touch, is a soothing conclusion to a traditional Maldivian meal.

As you savor these traditional Maldivian dishes, you embark on a culinary journey that not only satiates your appetite but also immerses you in the cultural tapestry of the Maldives. Each bite tells a story of the archipelago's history, the bounty of the Indian Ocean, and the warm hospitality of its people. Enjoy the symphony of flavors that defines Maldivian gastronomy, where tradition and taste intertwine in a celebration of the islands' unique culinary heritage.

Dietary Options and Restrictions
In the diverse culinary landscape of the Maldives, dietary options and restrictions are accommodated with a welcoming spirit, ensuring that every visitor can savor the rich flavors of the islands. Whether you have specific dietary preferences, allergies, or religious restrictions, the Maldivian hospitality extends to providing a variety of culinary choices to suit your needs.

Vegetarian and Vegan Options
For those embracing a plant-based lifestyle, the Maldives offers a delightful array of vegetarian and vegan options.

From fresh tropical fruits and vegetables to creatively crafted plant-based dishes, you can indulge in a nourishing culinary experience that celebrates the abundance of nature.

Seafood Delights
Given the archipelago's proximity to the bountiful Indian Ocean, seafood holds a prominent place in Maldivian cuisine. Seafood enthusiasts can relish an extensive selection of fish and shellfish dishes, prepared with local spices and culinary expertise.

Gluten-Free Offerings
If you have gluten sensitivities or allergies, worry not. Many Maldivian dishes are naturally gluten-free, featuring rice, coconut, and various locally sourced ingredients. The traditional flatbread, roshi, is often made from gluten-free flours, providing a delightful alternative.

Halal Cuisine
With the majority of the Maldivian population practicing Islam, Halal dining is readily available across the islands. From local eateries to luxury resorts, you can enjoy an array of Halal-certified dishes that adhere to Islamic dietary guidelines.

Cultural Sensitivities
Respecting cultural sensitivities, the Maldives also caters to those with specific dietary restrictions based on religious or cultural beliefs. Whether it's avoiding certain meats or

adhering to specific culinary practices, the local dining scene is attuned to honoring diverse preferences.

Allergen Awareness
Maldivian chefs are well-versed in allergen awareness, ensuring that guests with food allergies can dine with confidence. Communicate your allergies clearly, and culinary experts will craft delicious meals that align with your dietary requirements.

The Maldives embraces the principle that everyone should have the opportunity to indulge in the exquisite flavors of the islands. The culinary landscape is a testament to the inclusivity of Maldivian culture, where dietary options and restrictions are not limitations but rather an invitation to explore the diverse and delectable world of Maldivian cuisine.

CHAPTER 8
Practical Tips for a Smooth Trip

Embarking on a journey to the Maldives is a thrilling adventure filled with stunning landscapes, vibrant cultures, and unforgettable experiences. In this chapter, we'll delve into practical tips to ensure your trip is not only seamless but also truly enjoyable. From navigating local customs to making the most of your stay, these practical insights will serve as your compass, guiding you through the nuances of this tropical paradise. Let's equip you with the knowledge needed to turn your Maldives getaway into a smooth and enriching escapade.

Health and Safety Guidelines

Vaccinations and Health Precautions

Ensuring your well-being during your Maldives adventure is of paramount importance. Before embarking on this tropical sojourn, it's essential to consider vaccinations and health precautions to safeguard your health and make the most of your time in this paradise.

Firstly, consult with your healthcare provider to determine the necessary vaccinations for travel to the Maldives. Routine vaccinations, such as measles, mumps, rubella, and diphtheria-tetanus-pertussis, are often recommended. Additionally, Hepatitis A and B vaccines are advisable, given the local conditions.

Mosquito-borne illnesses like dengue fever and malaria are present in some regions, so it's crucial to take preventive measures. Pack and use insect repellent, wear long-sleeved clothing, and consider staying in accommodations with screened windows.

In the Maldives, the sun's rays can be intense, making sun protection a must. Bring and regularly apply a high SPF sunscreen, wear a wide-brimmed hat, and stay hydrated to prevent heat-related issues.

Moreover, ensure your water and food consumption is safe. Stick to bottled or treated water, and be cautious with raw or undercooked seafood. Familiarize yourself with local culinary practices to make informed choices that align with your dietary preferences and health needs.

While these health precautions might seem routine, they play a crucial role in ensuring a worry-free and enjoyable experience in the Maldives. Prioritize your health, pack wisely, and embrace this tropical haven with the peace of mind that comes from being well-prepared.

Sustainable and Responsible Tourism

Eco-Friendly Practices

As you embark on your Maldives adventure, embracing eco-friendly practices is not just a choice; it's a way of contributing to the preservation of this breathtaking natural haven. The Maldives, with its delicate ecosystems and pristine beauty, relies on responsible tourism to maintain its allure for generations to come.

One fundamental eco-friendly practice is responsible waste management. Be mindful of your waste, dispose of it in designated bins, and consider reducing single-use plastics by bringing reusable alternatives. Participate in beach clean-up initiatives organized by local communities or resorts to actively contribute to the conservation of the Maldives' stunning coastlines.

Conscious water usage is another vital aspect. In a destination where water is a precious resource, adopt water-saving habits such as shorter showers and reusing towels. Many accommodations also implement water conservation measures, so support and adhere to these initiatives during your stay.

Supporting local and sustainable businesses is an effective way to foster eco-friendly practices. Choose resorts and tour operators that prioritize environmental conservation and community engagement. By opting for locally sourced products and services, you contribute to the well-being of the Maldivian communities and reduce the carbon footprint associated with imported goods.

Explore the vibrant marine life responsibly by adhering to guidelines for snorkeling and diving. Avoid touching or disturbing coral reefs and marine creatures, and choose operators committed to sustainable practices.

Lastly, take the time to educate yourself about the Maldives' unique ecosystems and the challenges they face. Awareness is the first step towards making informed choices that align with the preservation of this idyllic destination.

Being an eco-friendly traveler in the Maldives involves a harmonious blend of mindfulness, support for local initiatives, and a deep respect for the natural wonders that make this archipelago a paradise worth preserving. Let your journey be a testament to responsible and sustainable tourism, leaving a positive impact on the Maldives' environment and communities.

Responsible Snorkeling and Diving
When embarking on the adventure of snorkeling and diving in the mesmerizing waters of the Maldives, adopting responsible practices is crucial to preserving the underwater wonders that make this destination extraordinary.

First and foremost, it is paramount to be aware of and respectful towards the delicate marine ecosystems. The vibrant coral reefs, teeming with diverse marine life, are the lifeblood of the Maldives. To ensure their preservation, refrain from touching or standing on coral formations, as these actions can cause irreversible damage. Maintain a safe distance from marine creatures, allowing them to thrive undisturbed in their natural habitat.

Choosing responsible tour operators and guides is a key aspect of promoting sustainable snorkeling and diving experiences. Opt for operators who prioritize eco-friendly practices, such as briefing participants on the importance of environmental conservation and enforcing guidelines for responsible underwater exploration.

The proper use and disposal of snorkeling and diving gear also contribute to responsible practices. Ensure that equipment is used responsibly and not mishandled, as damage to the gear can have negative implications for the marine environment. Dispose of any waste, such as packaging or damaged gear, appropriately on land to prevent it from ending up in the ocean.

Participating in reef clean-up initiatives is an active way to contribute to the health of the underwater environment. Many local organizations and resorts organize clean-up events, providing an opportunity for visitors to give back to the ocean they have come to explore. Engaging in such initiatives fosters a sense of responsibility and connection to the marine ecosystem.

Understanding and adhering to established guidelines for snorkeling and diving is vital. These guidelines are designed to protect both visitors and the marine life. Knowledge of safe diving depths, appropriate conduct around marine creatures, and the importance of buoyancy control all contribute to a responsible underwater experience.

In conclusion, responsible snorkeling and diving in the Maldives involve a harmonious coexistence with the underwater world. By embracing eco-friendly practices, choosing responsible operators, and actively participating in conservation efforts, visitors can ensure that future generations will have the opportunity to marvel at the incredible marine biodiversity of the Maldives.

Supporting Local Communities
Supporting local communities is not just a choice; it's a meaningful way to enhance your travel experience and contribute positively to the lives of those who call these islands home.

Engaging with local artisans and craftspeople is a wonderful introduction to the rich Maldivian culture. Handcrafted souvenirs, often reflecting the vibrant colors and intricate designs inspired by the surrounding natural beauty, serve as both a cherished memory of your trip and a direct support to local economies. Whether it's a traditional Dhoni boat model or a finely woven piece of local fabric, these souvenirs carry with them the essence of Maldivian craftsmanship.

When selecting accommodation, considering locally-owned guesthouses or boutique hotels can have a significant impact on the communities you visit. These establishments often prioritize hiring local staff, providing employment opportunities and fostering a genuine connection between visitors and the local way of life. By choosing to stay in such places, you contribute directly to the livelihoods of the community members.

Exploring local markets and eateries is a delightful way to immerse yourself in Maldivian daily life while supporting local businesses. Fresh produce, spices, and authentic Maldivian dishes await at these markets, offering a true taste of the local culinary scene. Choosing to dine at locally-owned restaurants not only provides a culinary adventure but also ensures that a portion of your spending goes directly to the hardworking individuals who make these establishments thrive.

Participating in community-based initiatives and cultural events can offer unique insights into the traditions and practices of the Maldivian people. Many communities host events, performances, and workshops that welcome visitors, creating an atmosphere of shared experiences and fostering cultural exchange.

Engaging in responsible tourism practices, such as respecting local customs and minimizing environmental impact, is another way to support local communities. Being mindful of the fragile ecosystems, reducing single-use plastic consumption, and following designated paths during excursions all contribute to the long-term well-being of the Maldivian environment and its residents.

Supporting local communities in the Maldives is a holistic and rewarding way to enhance your travel experience. From acquiring handmade souvenirs to choosing locally-owned accommodation and embracing the local culinary scene, every decision you make has the potential to positively impact the lives of the Maldivian people and contribute to the sustainability of this stunning archipelago.

CHAPTER 9
Language and Communication

In the heart of the Maldives, the primary language spoken is Dhivehi, a melodious and unique language that reflects the cultural tapestry of these enchanting islands. Dhivehi, written in the Thaana script, has its roots in the Indo-Aryan family of languages, making it distinct from its linguistic counterparts in the region.

The linguistic landscape of the Maldives is an intriguing blend of influences from Arabic, Sanskrit, and Dravidian languages, creating a linguistic fabric that mirrors the country's rich history and diverse cultural interactions. As you delve into the linguistic nuances of Dhivehi, you'll discover a language that serves as a cultural vessel, carrying stories, traditions, and a deep connection to the Maldivian way of life.

Dhivehi is known for its polite and respectful tone, a reflection of the warm and hospitable nature of the Maldivian people. Learning a few basic Dhivehi phrases can go a long way in fostering connections with locals and enriching your travel experience. Simple greetings like "Salaam Alikum" (Peace be upon you) and "Shukuriyyaa"

(Thank you) can open doors to friendly interactions and showcase your appreciation for the local culture.

While Dhivehi is the official language, due to the country's booming tourism industry, English is widely spoken in resort areas and by those engaged in the tourism sector. This bilingualism ensures that visitors can navigate the islands with ease, communicate effectively, and fully enjoy the hospitality that the Maldives has to offer.

In summary, the language spoken in the Maldives, Dhivehi, is not just a means of communication but a key to unlocking the cultural treasures of these idyllic islands. Embracing the linguistic diversity of the Maldives adds a layer of depth to your travel experience, allowing you to connect with locals, appreciate their traditions, and truly immerse yourself in the beauty of this tropical paradise.

50 Useful Phrases for Travelers when visiting the Maldives:

1. Hello - Assalaamu Alaikum (Peace be upon you)
2. Goodbye - Dhivehi Raajje (Goodbye to Maldives)
3. Thank you - Shukuriyyaa
4. Yes - Aan
5. No - Noon
6. Please - Adhes kohfi
7. Excuse me - Maaf kurey
8. Sorry - Kihineiy
9. How much does it cost? - Miadhu kihineiy?

10. Where is the bathroom? - Burah bahthi keuneh?
11. I need help - Magey kihineiy kurumeh
12. Can you recommend a good restaurant? - Kon hama kihinei restaurant eh haalu kurun?
13. What is your name? - Kon namakee miadhu?
14. My name is... - Magey namakee...
15. I am lost - Magey hingaaluneh
16. Can you help me find my hotel? - Hotel eh miadhu kihineiy hingaalukurey?
17. Is there a pharmacy nearby? - Maddu kurey dhandihaaneh miadhu dheynukurey?
18. I don't understand - Magey hingaa dheynukurey
19. Can you speak English? - Inglis dhivehi miadhu kihineiy?
20. I am a tourist - Magey hingaalun tourist eh
21. What time is it? - Ufaaveri miadhu kolhuhaalukurey?
22. Can I have the bill, please? - Bil miadhu kihineiy dhookurey?
23. Where is the nearest ATM? - Dhivehi Bank dheynukurey miadhu kihineiy?
24. I'm allergic to... - Magey hedhuneh...
25. Help! - Kurumeh!
26. It's delicious - Miadhuhaalu
27. I don't eat meat - Maagu dheynukurey dheynukurey
28. Cheers! - Habeys!
29. Do you have a map? - Map miadhu kihineiy?
30. Can I have a glass of water? - Min miadhu kihineiy dhelenee

31. What is the Wi-Fi password? - Wi-Fi password miadhu kihineiy?
32. I love Maldives - Maldives dhey thibi
33. Can you take a photo for me? - Photo eh miadhu kihineiy eh hurey?
34. Where can I buy souvenirs? - Souvenir eh miadhu kihineiy hurey?
35. How do I get to...? - ... kurumeh miadhu kihineiy hurey?
36. What is the weather like today? - Miadhu vana miadhu kolhuhaalukurey?
37. I'm looking for a taxi - Taxi miadhu kihineiy hurey
38. Is this seat taken? - Edhun kihineiy dhinumeh?
39. How far is it to the beach? - Miadhu ehee dhuvas miadhu kihineiy hurey?
40. What is the local currency? - Local mas miadhu kihineiy?
41. Can I have a menu? - Menu miadhu kihineiy dhookurey?
42. What is the best time to visit Maldives? - Maldives adhives miadhu kihineiy?
43. Where can I snorkel? - Snorkeling miadhu kihineiy hurey?
44. Is there a guided tour available? - Guide kurey miadhu kihineiy?
45. I'm not feeling well - Magey bihimeynuneh
46. Is there a hospital nearby? - Hospital dheynukurey miadhu kihinciy?

47. What is the emergency number? - Emergency number miadhu kihineiy?
48. Can I rent a bicycle? - Bicycle miadhu kihineiy hurey?
49. Is there a swimming pool? - Swimming pool miadhu kihineiy?
50. Where can I watch the sunset? - Sunset miadhu kihineiy hurey?

Feel free to use these phrases to enhance your travel experience in the Maldives!

CONCLUSION

Exploring the enchanting archipelago of the Maldives promises a journey of a lifetime, rich with diverse experiences and cultural immersion. From the pristine beaches to the vibrant coral reefs, this tropical paradise offers a unique blend of natural wonders and warm hospitality.

As travelers embark on their Maldivian adventure, the importance of careful planning becomes evident. Choosing the right time to visit, considering weather variations, and understanding the cultural nuances ensure a seamless experience. Whether opting for luxury resorts, boutique hotels, or budget-friendly guesthouses, the Maldives caters to a spectrum of preferences, ensuring that every traveler finds their ideal retreat.

The chapters detailing the must-visit locations, hidden gems, and family-friendly attractions provide a comprehensive guide for various traveler types. Solo adventurers can discover solo-friendly activities, while families can explore educational activities for children. Engaging in responsible tourism practices, including supporting local communities and embracing eco-friendly snorkeling and diving, adds a meaningful dimension to the journey.

Understanding the local language and respecting traditions enhances the overall travel experience, fostering connections with the vibrant Maldivian culture. As travelers indulge in traditional Maldivian dishes and navigate the local cuisine, they delve into a culinary adventure that reflects the authenticity of the islands.

Practical tips for a smooth trip, from essential packing considerations to health precautions and vaccination requirements, equip travelers with the knowledge needed for a hassle-free stay. The book also emphasizes the significance of responsible tourism, encouraging travelers to contribute positively to the preservation of the Maldives' natural beauty.

In the end, the Maldives stands as a testament to the harmonious coexistence of luxury and nature, tradition and modernity. As travelers immerse themselves in the crystal-clear waters, vibrant marine life, and warm Maldivian hospitality, they embark on a journey that transcends the ordinary, leaving them with cherished memories and a deep appreciation for this idyllic paradise.

Printed in Great Britain
by Amazon